"This beautiful book by Michael and Christiana reminds us that the entire creation is groaning, aching for a new world, like a mother giving birth. Pregnancy means labor, sweat, tears, blood . . . but in the end it also means new life! So roll up your sleeves and get ready . . . a new world is coming. We get to be the midwives."

Shane Claiborne, author and activist

"In an over-messaged world, *To Alter Your World* cuts through noise with compelling narrative that describes our invitation to participate in kingdom transformation as a midwifing process rather than an engineering one. In a world experiencing searing pain with ever-deepening fault lines of injustice and income inequality, Christiana and Michael call us to question our traditional starting points for mission. With the stakes so high, they urge us to tap into Christ's imagination rather than summon our human determination. This is a wonderfully insightful book that honestly recounts sobering realities but also hopefully describes encouraging signs of how God is at work among us."

John Hayes, author of *Submerge* and Founder of InnerCHANGE

"In this outstanding book, my comrade Michael Frost further develops his pioneering ideas on how we ought to follow the way of our incarnate Lord—only here he partners with an exemplary practitioner of incarnational mission, Christiana Rice. The result is a piece of writing that is as illuminating as it is inspiring. Wonderful!"

Alan Hirsch, founder, 100Movements, Forge Mission Training Network, Future Travelers, coauthor of *The Permanent Revolution*

"Rejecting withdrawal or simply joining with the world, Frost and Rice ask the question all over again: How can we Christians transform the world? Moving beyond the old, tired Christendom habits, they offer the church a fresh way to inhabit, take up roots, and let God birth his kingdom in the neighborhoods of our lives. Their book *To Alter Your World* truly alters our imagination for the practice of church, and I am so pleased to recommend it."

David Fitch, B. R. Lindner Chair of Evangelical Theology, Northern Seminary, pastor, Peace of Christ Church, Westmont, Illinois

"A bold and beautiful call to steward God's good news for the world. A must-read for anyone who longs to wade into the deep and ride the current to personal and global redemption. A deeply biblical glimpse of a deeply personal God inviting us into a deeply beautiful journey."

Danielle Strickland, speaker, author of *A Beautiful Mess*

"Most of us ache to see our messed-up world altered for the good, yet too often we unintentionally create more problems by pushing our own agendas. In *To Alter Your World*, Mike and Christiana give us an insightful and timely metaphor that helps us detect the impulses of the Spirit so we can humbly inhabit our neighborhoods and birth new kingdom realities."

JR Woodward, national director, V3 Church Planting Movement, coauthor of *The Church as Movement*

"One of the many things I love about *To Alter Your World* is how Rice and Frost encourage the readers to see themselves as those who will actually partner with God to help birth a wonderful new world. What an awesome and humbling responsibility!"

Majora Carter, urban revitalization strategist and public radio host

"Pioneers. Adventurers. Explorers. Leaders. Missiologists. Those are the words that commonly come to mind when we consider our role as we engage with the Great Commisson in post-Christian contexts. But midwives? Seriously? Yes. They stand at the threshold of new life in all its raw vulnerability and potential. Occasionally they stand tenderly alongside the grieving, mourning lost joy and promise. Leading with sacrifice and strength, their role is never about them; they're simply present to serve as needed. In this book, Frost and Rice recognize that as we engage with what God is birthing in our world, a fresh posture is required. Yep, it's time to call the midwife; our world is waiting."

Jo Saxton, author of *More Than Enchanting*

TO

PARTNERING WITH
GOD TO REBIRTH
OUR COMMUNITIES

ALTER
YOUR
WORLD

MICHAEL FROST / CHRISTIANA RICE

IVP Books

An imprint of InterVarsity Press
Downers Grove, Illinois

InterVarsity Press
P.O. Box 1400, Downers Grove, IL 60515-1426
ivpress.com
email@ivpress.com

InterVarsity Press® is the book-publishing division of InterVarsity Christian Fellowship/USA®, a movement of students and faculty active on campus at hundreds of universities, colleges and schools of nursing in the United States of America, and a member movement of the International Fellowship of Evangelical Students. For information about local and regional activities, visit intervarsity.org.

Scripture quotations, unless otherwise noted, are from the New Revised Standard Version of the Bible, copyright 1989 by the Division of Christian Education of the National Council of the Churches of Christ in the USA. Used by permission. All rights reserved.

While any stories in this book are true, some names and identifying information may have been changed to protect the privacy of individuals.

Cover design: Cindy Kiple
Interior design: Jeanna Wiggins
Images: graphic buildings: © Diane Labombarbe/iStockphoto
abstract texture: © 13UG13th/iStockphoto
Figure 7.3: Mark Wallinger's Ecce Homo, Fourth Plinth, Trafalgar Square, photo by Dangerpuss, Guardian Witness
Figure 9.1: image by Philip Straub

ISBN 978-0-8308-4137-0 (print)
ISBN 978-0-8308-9335-5 (digital)

Printed in the United States of America ♾

Library of Congress Cataloging-in-Publication Data
Names: Frost, Michael, 1961- author.
Title: To alter your world : partnering with God to rebirth our communities /
    Michael Frost and Christiana Rice.
Description: Downers Grove : InterVarsity Press, 2017. | Includes
    bibliographical references.
Identifiers: LCCN 2016046966 (print) | LCCN 2016052452 (ebook) | ISBN
    9780830841370 (pbk. : alk. paper) | ISBN 9780830893355 (eBook)
Subjects: LCSH: Church and the world. | Christianity--Influence. |
    Change--Religious aspects--Christianity. | Redemption--Christianity. |
    Mission of the church. | Communities--Religious aspects--Christianity.
Classification: LCC BR115.W6 F76 2016 (print) | LCC BR115.W6 (ebook) | DDC
    266--dc23
LC record available at https://lccn.loc.gov/2016046966
A catalog record for this book is available from the Library of Congress.

P   25   24   23   22   21   20   19   18   17   16   15   14   13   12   11   10   9   8   7   6   5   4   3   2   1

Y   34   33   32   31   30   29   28   27   26   25   24   23   22   21   20   19   18   17

We dedicate this book to

those heroic people around the globe

whose stories are told in these pages.

At great personal cost they have embraced

the selfless calling of Christ to serve the poor,

to love their neighbors, to create space at their tables,

and to help shape communities of faith

that alter their worlds.

*What we actually need is to imagine that
God is up to something. Imagine that
God is active in the midst of what seems to be
an unremitting unraveling of not just our
churches but our way of life in North America....
We are invited to embrace a fundamentally
different reality where God is remaking
the world and we are called to participate
in that remaking.*

ALAN ROXBURGH

CONTENTS

INTRODUCTION

In our post-Christendom, pluralistic context, how should those who follow Christ engage the public sphere? In the eyes of its detractors, the church's current forays into culture-shaping can be seen merely as argumentative and whiny at best, or privileged and triumphalist at worst. The church's public attempts to reclaim societal influence can appear to be about regaining power and control, something which is completely at odds with the self-emptying example of Christ.

And yet, while this may be an accurate assessment of some church rhetoric, it certainly doesn't represent the much wider, more subversive transforming presence of Jesus followers in the world. Why is there such disparity and misrepresentation of the Christian community in the public arena? And how can Christians better represent the true mission of God to reconcile the world?

One of our greatest challenges as the church of tomorrow lies in finding the balance between retaining our missional particularity and humbly interacting as one perspective and voice among many. Our task is not to grope for cultural dominance, but to build bonds of peace and collaboration. To participate in God's ongoing work of renewal in the world, we believe the church needs a fresh vision for and model of Christian partnership in these partisan times.

That will require a shift from combative discourse (*para-logos*) to the dialectical exchange of our deepest world-forming narratives (*dia-logos*). It will include learning how to resist our impulses to separate, segregate and condemn, in order to embrace the power of collaboration without compromising our convictions as Christ followers. We're convinced this shift will unearth the wisdom that serves holistic human flourishing and, by God's grace, bring together the disparate factions in society—including the church—to join God's world-altering movement toward a truly common good in the here and now.

So, how do a missiologist from Sydney, Australia, and an urban missionary from San Diego, California, end up collaborating on a book about the church's contribution to altering the world? Don't ask us—we're just as surprised as anyone. While we have several mutual friends and our paths have crossed at various events and conferences over the years, the idea to write together seemed to emerge spontaneously and come to fruition unexpectedly and remarkably easily.

It seems like an obvious collaboration when you think about it. Christiana is a local practitioner. She leads a grassroots faith community in the Golden Hill neighborhood of San Diego, as well as teaching, coaching and leading people who desire to see Christ's transformation in their lives and on their streets. And Michael is a seminary professor who has been writing and speaking about a missional paradigm for the church for many years, as well as leading a missional community, Small Boat Big Sea, in the Manly neighborhood of Sydney. In other words, one is a practitioner who teaches, and the other is a teacher who practices.

We met years ago at a Missio training event in Denver, and have been involved in the development of the Parish Collective's annual Inhabit Conference in Seattle. Through those interactions it became obvious we share a passion for God's mission, incarnational living, leadership development and experiencing and expressing God's restoration in local contexts. The book you're holding represents not only our thinking on the culture-altering work of Christ and his people, but also it emerges from the mistakes we've made and the successes God has granted us in our respective communities. It also includes many of our friends' stories about engaging with culture in places such as Cape Town, South Africa; Karlsruhe, Germany; Vancouver, Canada; Sioux Falls, South Dakota; El Paso, Texas; and elsewhere.

We are convinced that God is at work across the globe, reconciling the world to the divine order and giving us this ministry of reconciliation. As part of God's world-changing work of reconciliation we are invited to be, as Lesslie Newbigin once wrote, a sign—an instrument and a foretaste of that reconciled world. As part of our dialogical, collaborative engagement in society we are signposts to the new world God is ushering in, instruments through which God answers our prayer for that new world to come, and a real, flesh-and-blood, locally rooted taste of the new heavens and new earth.

Whenever we talk to our students or the people we mentor and lead about this vision for the church in society, we sense they are greatly stimulated by our discussion. Innumerable others are thinking about the same things and longing for communities through which to live out these God-breathed dreams and hopes. Yet the challenges of moving in this direction and making the necessary adjustments to be a sign, instrument and foretaste of the new creation are considerable and costly. Church business-as-usual will not adequately lead to congregations influencing society, joining forces with their neighbors and being open to learn from others. It is our hope that this book might contribute, even if ever so slightly, to helping churches take the leap into their true identity and fulfill their destiny to alter their world and be the people God intended for us to be.

1

GOD GROANS LIKE A WOMAN IN LABOR

For a long time I have held my peace,
I have kept still and restrained myself;
now I will cry out like a woman in labor,
I will gasp and pant.

ISAIAH 42:14

Israel longed for God to speak. They were enduring the humiliation and dislocation of exile in Babylon, and they needed a new word, just a fragment of hope. False prophets had predicted their exile would be short-lived, that Babylon would fall, Jerusalem would be saved, and the people would soon return home. But theirs was a fictitious hope. There seemed no indication that they would soon return to the land of their forebears. The prophet Jeremiah counseled them that Babylon would be this generation's only home. He called on them to settle in the land of their enemies, to work that land and "build houses . . . plant gardens and eat what they produce" (Jer 29:5). So they stayed, attempting to make a home among their captors, desiring a fresh vision from God that a new world was coming.

And finally through another prophet, Isaiah, God begins to speak: "For a long time I have held my peace, I have kept still and restrained myself." The word that comes to them through Isaiah is breathtaking. Its imagery is profound. And surprising. "Now I will cry out like a woman in labor, I will gasp and pant," declares Yahweh (Is 42:14).

It is the stunning announcement that God, groaning like a woman in labor, will soon give birth to new life.

It's an unexpected metaphor for God because in the ancient world no one was more vulnerable than a birthing mother. The instances of death during childbirth were high. Giving birth in the ancient world wasn't as it is today. Women squatted, kneeled or stood on brightly painted birthing bricks around a hole in the ground. Those from more affluent families gave birth on a specially made birthing chair with a hole in the seat. Both these practices were common among Jewish women in biblical times as well.

Like a vulnerable woman in the final stages of labor, God's silence during Israel's defeat and captivity had been taken for powerlessness. But God's seeming absence wasn't weakness. It was gestation. Now, Yahweh will cry out as if in labor, birthing a new future for them.

In fact, while a woman might be at greater risk during labor, her apparent helplessness shouldn't be taken as anything less than the extraordinary power to bring forth life. This is the metaphor God chooses to describe the profaned absence the people of Israel had experienced in exile, and it beautifully describes the work of God throughout the ages—showing strength through weakness.

Some people today have referred to the church's current situation in the West as being a kind of exile. Christians haven't been carried to a new land, but the culture around them has changed. It is not uncommon for Christians to feel as though they're building their houses and planting their gardens on foreign soil. It's as if the land beneath the church's feet has shifted over recent generations and they feel a desperate need to hear Yahweh's voice, to know the way forward, to trust in God's promises for the future.

The world today is clearly foreign soil for us. As we write, the self-described Islamic State is beheading Christians in Libya and Syria. Health professionals are laboring to control an Ebola pandemic in West Africa. America is struggling to deal with a child-migrant crisis. We live with the chronic brokenness of domestic violence, child sexual assault, family breakdown, oppression of the weak, dirty politics, unfair business practices, racism, extreme poverty, dishonest government, murder, theft, environmental degradation and many other indicators of the fissures and fractures that run through the heart of everything.

Nations are constantly at war. Societies are continually distressed. There's a deep yearning for a different way to educate our children, and a hunger for a new way of conducting business and politics. No one believes that continuing on this same trajectory will make a difference in the healing of the world.

Like exiled Israel, the church today yearns for a word from God. As Christians, we believe that Christ came into the world to bring a new order; to bring redemption, healing and restoration; and to birth a new society of redeemed persons. And as that new society, we hold fast to the truth that God is directing history toward its true end. But like Israel, we need to hear afresh that God is at work. We need to be reminded that, though forces of chaos and evil seem evident, God groans like a woman in labor, giving birth to the new world promised throughout the generations and confirmed for us in Christ.

We believe that the life, death and resurrection of Jesus invite all of humanity to enter deeply into the needs of a broken world and to join God as agents of the renewal, restoration and reconciliation of all things in readiness for the age to come. Furthermore, we would suggest that it's not so much our task to change the world as it is to be that part of the world that is already being birthed by Christ. As Bishop Lesslie Newbigin says,

> The Bible, then, is covered with God's purpose of blessing for all the nations. It is concerned with the completion of God's purpose in the creation of the world and of man within the world. It is not—to put it crudely—concerned with offering a way of escape for the redeemed soul out of history, but with the action of God to bring history to its true end.[1]

Rather than enjoining another contest for the right legislation, or capitulating to our borderline status, we believe it is possible to join God's world-birthing enterprise by inhabiting and engaging at a central but grassroots level. God's redemptive plan invites us to inhabit neighborhoods, towns and villages in the way of Jesus, to live wholeheartedly into our vocational calling and, there, to join God's work of making all things just and whole. This is a monumental task, one not easily undertaken and one we embrace with no confidence that we can achieve it in our lifetimes. It is a task bigger than us and even bigger than the work of the church. As Newbigin says, it is the *action of God* to bring history to its true end. And we are invited to love and serve God as agents, sowing the seeds of renewal in the contaminated soil of a broken world. N. T. Wright describes our work this way:

> Our task, as image-bearing, God-loving, Christ-shaped, Spirit-filled Christians, following Christ and shaping our world, is to announce redemption to a world that has discovered its fallenness, to announce healing to a world that has discovered

its brokenness, to proclaim love and trust to the world that knows only exploitation, fear and suspicion.[2]

As followers of Jesus, we learn to receive and demonstrate redemption, healing, love and trust in the ordinary, everyday beauty and brokenness of life here on earth. Coming together as communities of faith and reconciliation, we embody our sacramental calling to be a sign of the new creation God is giving birth to in the world. This is our collective identity. And by it and through it we join God's work to alter this world and to anticipate the next.

While the false prophets of Israel urged the Babylonian captives not to put down roots but to stay on their toes, ready for their impending departure, the true sons and daughters of God know that God's reign is not something we can quickly achieve in our own strength. If God is groaning like a woman in labor, and if a new world is being born before our very eyes, being pushed forth through the cracks of our broken world, our job isn't to hurry it along. Rather our job is to join God and partner with him in the delivery room and to stop imagining we can birth the new world with our own strategies and methodologies. Indeed, our attempts to usher in the new order in recent years haven't produced the kind of restoration, redemption or reconciliation in this world that we believe God envisions.

RELIGIOUS AND POLITICAL ACTIVITY ALONE WON'T BIRTH A NEW WORLD

For the past half century the church in America has put its culture-shaping energy into a broadly two-pronged approach of planting and growing churches, and entering the political process, particularly on certain moral ethical issues. It is as if we've believed that more and bigger churches and better legislation could birth a new world. So, how's that been working out for us? How well has the suffering of nations been relieved through this particular vision? Well, frankly, on the whole, not that well.

For example, recent research tells us that wealth inequality has widened significantly along racial and ethnic lines since the end of the Great Recession. The wealth of white households was thirteen times the median wealth of black households in 2013, compared with eight times the wealth in 2010.[3] That's the biggest gap since 1989, when whites had seventeen times the wealth of black households. Is this the world as God intends it?

Furthermore, the 2014 riots in Ferguson, Missouri, highlighted what Ed Stetzer said was, "the important if seldom acknowledged truth that racism is still present and deep-seated among many in our culture."[4] In a *Christianity Today* blog, Pastor Leonce Crump writes, "We live in an oppressive system, strategically engineered to subvert the progress of entire people groups and benefit the progress of another. This is the injustice."[5] In response to Crump's blog, Stetzer remarked, "Many godly African American leaders are hurting and they are explaining why. I think we should listen to them."[6]

Listening is certainly the first step, and surely we agree that the abuse of privilege and power is not a mark of the world that God is giving birth to. In her book *The New Jim Crow*, civil rights activist Michelle Alexander writes, "If we want to put an end to the history of racial caste in America—we must lay down our racial bribes, join hands with people of all colors who are not content to wait for change to trickle down, and say to those who would stand in our way: Accept all of us or none."[7] Our listening must lead to enacting the good news of Jesus in ways that revolutionize society and bring freedom for all, not just for some.

Add to this recent examples of mass shootings across America and it's obvious that the United States has a problem with violence, where there are an estimated 283 million guns in civilian hands. In fact, more than 30,000 people are killed by firearms each year in this country. That's more than thirty people each day, half of them between the ages of eighteen and thirty-five. Homicide is the primary cause of death among African Americans of that age group.[8]

And if firearm deaths aren't concerning enough, we are in the grip of an epidemic of domestic violence against women. One in four women report experiencing violence at the hands of their intimate partner. As Soraya Chemaly points out, in an age of anxiety about terrorism, "statistically speaking, an American woman has as much a chance of being killed by her own furniture as being hit in a terrorist attack." Strangulation at the hands of a husband or boyfriend is even more common, so much so that the *Washington Post* called it the "gateway to murder." To put it in context, more than 6,800 US troops were killed in combat in Afghanistan and Iraq.[9] In the same period (from 2001 to 2012), the number of women killed as the result of domestic violence in the United States was 11,766.[10]

If you need further evidence that our world needs healing, a recent report found that one in thirty American children are homeless. That translates to 2.5 million children living in shelters, neighbors' basements, cars, campgrounds and worse—a marked increase on previous rates. Racial disparities, increasing poverty and domestic violence were identified as responsible for the historic high.[11]

Despite a generation of political opposition by Christians to abortion there were still over one million terminations performed in the United States in 2011. Interestingly, while the abortion rate has been dropping somewhat since 2000, abortions have increased 18 percent among poor women, while decreasing 28 percent among higher-income women.[12]

We could recount instances of disadvantage, cruelty, discrimination and hatred. Our point is simply that we are not living in the world that God desires. It feels like exile. But fear not, God is crying out like a woman in labor, gasping and panting out a different future to the one we currently endure. Reducing the culture-altering work

of God's people to church growth and political lobbying has not
shifted the trajectory of society in any marked ways. And yet the
American church continues to pour time, energy and money into
trying to turn the tide on the decline in their attendance and membership and the diminishing lifespan of new church plants. Should
this really be our primary concern? We believe our calling is more
ambitious, more dynamic, more daring than that.

Our social media feeds frequently feature blogs and articles
about why young people are leaving the church. While the statistics
on the numbers of people who come from Christian homes and
have now either left the church or denied the beliefs of their up-
bringing aren't good, maybe focusing on why they're leaving is actually contributing to driving them away. If the church spent more
time on actually being what it should be, and less time on figuring
out whether millennials are lazy or self-centered or whatever,
perhaps the problem wouldn't be so great. In other words, stop
trying to work out what's wrong with church-leavers and start
looking at where the church has gone wrong. As Carlos Rodriguez
puts it, "Somehow the *pro-guns, anti-abortion, immigrants-are-
bad, only-Conservatives-know Jesus* approach, is causing us to lose
what God values more . . . souls."[13]

In saying this, Rodriguez isn't suggesting a watering down of
biblical values. He's speaking about a culture of militancy that has
become distasteful to younger Christians. His article was written
in response to actor Jennifer Lawrence's criticisms of the Kentucky
church she grew up in. He quotes Lawrence as referring to people
holding crucifixes like pitchforks, fighting the good fight. That's a
startling image, and whether it's fair or not, it has become a broadly
held caricature of Christians today. We think many younger Christians would agree with pastor and blogger John Pavlovitz's summary,
"If you can't affirm what you believe without belittling what someone
else does, then you have a lousy testimony."[14]

WITHDRAWAL FROM POST-CHRISTIAN SOCIETY

More recently, other voices have been calling on the church to abandon its combative stance toward society, to recognize that we now live in a post-Christian culture and to withdraw to the margins as a kind of community-in-exile. For example, in response to the Supreme Court's 2015 gay marriage decision, conservative blogger and author Rod Dreher declared it was time for Christians to strategically retreat from center stage and embrace their marginal status where they could keep "the light of faith burning through the surrounding cultural darkness." He continued: "We have to accept that we really are living in a culturally post-Christian nation. The fundamental norms Christians have long been able to depend on no longer exist."[15]

English writer Mark Woods weighed in on the discussion, explaining that European Christians have long embraced their peripheral status in society and calling on American conservatives to wake up and smell the coffee: "Evangelicals are going to have to get used to living in a society which is no longer as congenial to them as once it was."[16] He went on to commend a two-tiered system in which Christians could choose to define marriage one way, while the state defines it another. In other words, the church would be a marginal, alternative community, extolling the benefits and blessings of their approach over and against the state.

This approach seems appealing to many people who are tired of the combative stance many in the Religious Right have adopted. When socially conservative Christians railed against the Supreme Court's Obergefell decision legalizing gay marriage by calling it the *Roe v. Wade* of marriage, there was a collective groan from many moderate and progressive Christians. Another battle? Another culture war like the last one, even though that battle saw no victory for conservative Christian values? Either battle-weary or just weary of others battling, many Christians find some solace in the idea of withdrawal to the edges to find purpose as exiles in post-Christendom.

But Jeremiah's prophecy to the Babylonian captives wasn't to hunker down at the edges of society and wait it all out. The word from God through Jeremiah was this:

> This is what the LORD Almighty, the God of Israel, says to all those I carried into exile from Jerusalem to Babylon: "Build houses and settle down; plant gardens and eat what they produce. Marry and have sons and daughters; find wives for your sons and give your daughters in marriage, so that they too may have sons and daughters. Increase in number there; do not decrease. Also, seek the peace and prosperity of the city to which I have carried you into exile. Pray to the LORD for it, because if it prospers, you too will prosper." (Jer 29:4-7 NIV)

The exiles were called neither to fight Babylonian culture, nor to retreat from it. They were urged to *inhabit* it. We think this is the way for the church today, too. It's a third way between fighting and retreating. We believe it is not time for the church to retreat, but to lean into the rhythms of the societies we are an integral part of, recognizing our shared humanity with others. Only then can we truly be catalysts for transformation and, like salt and light, shift the cultural values slowly but surely as a participatory community of grace, love and mercy.

Recently, we were delighted to read *New York Times* columnist David Brooks urging "social conservatives" outraged by the Obergefell decision to engage a different strategy to the old culture wars approach. We think his advice holds for both moderate and progressive Christians as well:

> We live in a society plagued by formlessness and radical flux, in which bonds, social structures and commitments are strained and frayed. Millions of kids live in stressed and fluid

living arrangements. Many communities have suffered a loss of social capital. Many young people grow up in a sexual and social environment rendered barbaric because there are no common norms. Many adults hunger for meaning and goodness, but lack a spiritual vocabulary to think things through.

Social conservatives could be the people who help reweave the sinews of society. They already subscribe to a faith built on selfless love. They can serve as examples of commitment. They are equipped with a vocabulary to distinguish right from wrong, what dignifies and what demeans. They already, but in private, tithe to the poor and nurture the lonely.

The defining face of social conservatism could be this: Those are the people who go into underprivileged areas and form organizations to help nurture stable families. Those are the people who build community institutions in places where they are sparse. Those are the people who can help us think about how economic joblessness and spiritual poverty reinforce each other. Those are the people who converse with us about the transcendent in everyday life.[17]

In other words, as he puts it, more Dorothy Day than Franklin Graham; more Salvation Army than Moral Majority. Brooks does not publicly identify as a Christian, yet he is calling the church to do precisely what we are commending—to repair a society torn apart by dissension, wracked by hatred, numbed by carelessness. Christian moralism has gotten us nowhere. In fact, the church has spent more energy developing a moral code that we can't fully prove and which none of us thoroughly lives by (try though we might) than we have simply sought to love our neighbors as ourselves. God is love, and only God holds the wisdom of perfect love. No moral code is going to get us closer to that love.

Do Christians believe Jesus has an answer for racism and racial inequality? Do we think the Bible provides responses to a world of violence, both domestic and international? Does it involve more than just inviting people to a church service? Of course it does! But perhaps our missiology is stunted and our imagination shallow as we envision the future of the church. The redemptive plan of God cannot be divorced from the fruitfulness of the church. As the world is redeemed, the church flourishes; and as the church flourishes, the world is redeemed. So, the church is both commissioned and equipped to repair the fabric of society, and to serve as envoys of love, dignity, commitment, communion and grace. As David Bosch wrote,

> The central theme of our missionary message is that Christ is risen, and that, secondly and consequently, the church is called to live the resurrection life in the here and now and to be a sign of contradiction against the forces of death and destruction.[18]

This book is about satisfying the desire to see the church altering the trajectory of culture in the way God envisions. To do so will involve new ways of thinking about community, politics, business, education, health care, art, religion and society itself. It will involve everyone, not just the clergy. It will involve not merely asking what kind of church the world needs, but what kind of a world God is giving birth to.

WHAT IS GOD GIVING BIRTH TO?

We recognize the metaphor of God panting like a woman in labor is a disturbing one for some readers. There are reasonable concerns about using feminine imagery for God, based on their similarities to pagan ways of talking about the divine feminine. We find theologian Elizabeth Achtemeier helpful in this respect. Acknowledging the patriarchal and exclusive ways language has been used by the church, she nonetheless cautions us about appearing to suggest God is feminine:

> First, it is universally recognized by biblical scholars that the God of the Bible has no sexuality. Sexuality is a structure of creation (cf. Gen. 1-2), confined within the limits of the creation (cf. Matt. 22:30), and the God of the Bible is consistently pictured as totally other than all creation.[19]

We agree. And we are not proposing we all start praying to "Mother God," which, while not technically impossible to say, is fraught with theological controversy. The reference in Isaiah, quoted earlier, is a metaphor describing the *work* of God among the Hebrews during the time of exile. Biblical metaphors for God as a birthing woman or a warrior or an eagle aren't offered as descriptors of the *nature* of God, but as ways for us to see the activity of God in our midst. Therefore, the various feminine similes found in Scripture are very useful for us in trying to grasp the fullness and beauty of the biblical God. Theologian Elizabeth Johnson is helpful on this:

> The mystery of God is properly understood as neither male nor female but transcends both in an unimaginable way. But insofar as God creates both male and female in the divine image and is the source of the perfections in both, either can be equally well used as metaphor to point to divine mystery. Both in fact are needed for less inadequate speech about God, in whose image the human race is created. This "clue" for speaking of God in the image of male and female has the advantage of making clear at the outset that women enjoy the dignity of being made in God's image and are therefore as capable as men of representing God.[20]

But further to this, as Achtemeier explains, the God of the Bible is not identified with creation as in other religions, lest human beings are inclined to worship that creation rather than the Creator (see Rom 1:25). Essentially any imagery of creation having come from the "womb" of God cuts deeply across the very important Hebrew emphasis on that distinction between Creator and the created. It is no accident that such imagery is rare in Hebrew literature. It could have opened the door to all kinds of pagan interpretations. Achtemeier says,

> The God of the Bible is sharply distinguished from everything that he has made. To be sure, God works in his creation through the instruments of his Word and Spirit; he orders his creation and sustains it; he constantly cares for it; but he is never identified with it. And it is that holiness, that otherness, that transcendence of the Creator, which also distinguishes biblical religion from all others.[21]

Acknowledging that, we would argue that Isaiah 42:14 isn't referring to God's work as Creator, but to God's activity in "birthing" the new creation, the alternate reality to the brutishness and humiliation of the exile. God is genderless. And God is distinguished from creation. But the reign of God proceeds from God's holy and gracious nature. It is a reflection of Yahweh's divine character; the evidences of it here on earth, we would say, are birthed by God, not by us. This was a hard lesson for the Babylonian exiles, as it is for us. Just as they were powerless to end their exile and were forced to submit to God's timetable, so we today need to learn we cannot speed the coming of God's kingdom by our own activity, whether ecclesial or political. We are merely God's attendants, God's servants, responding to the arrival of the world we were promised.

Wanting to change the world quickly is understandable. Impatiently organizing our energies and marshaling our forces seems reasonable. But there are grave dangers when all that activity drifts into trying to take control of God's agenda. This is a book about changing the world. But it's also a book about patiently listening to

God, taking our cues from the unfurling of God's reign, staying in step with the Spirit's agenda, and joining the triune God as colaborers in the work of the kingdom.

Daniel was an exile in Babylon. He embodied this mission perfectly. Brought into the palace of the Chaldean King Nebuchadnezzar II, Daniel was to enjoy enormous privilege and opportunity (and court great danger and near death at times), rising effectively to the role of prime minister of the empire. This was no mean feat for a Hebrew exile. Through what Old Testament scholar Walter Brueggemann calls "an endlessly cunning, risky process of negotiation,"[22] Daniel lives an uneasy life of balancing between resistance and embrace among the Babylonians, all the while relying on Yahweh's faithful presence with him.

In Daniel 7, during the reign of Nebuchadnezzar's successor, Belshazzar, Daniel has a bizarre dream of ghastly beasts rising up from a great sea. These four monsters represent the great empires of the Ancient Near East—Babylon, Medo-Persia, Greece and finally Rome, the worst of all. By playing this terrifying scene across the landscape of his imagination, God serves to reveal to Daniel the true nature of human empire. It is beastly, cruel and capricious.

Since Babylon and Rome, history has seen empires like Nazi Germany, the Soviet Union, Mao Zedong's China and Pol Pot's Cambodia come and go. Today we live with the despotic North Korean empire of Kim Jong-un and the dramatic rise of the self-described Islamic State.

In Daniel's dream the stranglehold of the empire wasn't broken by the efforts of Daniel or his fellow exiles. The four beasts he sees appear to be insurmountable, unstoppable, all-powerful. No amount of effort by the exiled Hebrews could have made any difference to Babylon, just as no amount of human effort by the early church could have brought Rome to its knees. Ultimately, they are defeated by the sheer, unadulterated power of God's reign. In Daniel 7, we are offered a glimpse of the majesty of God:

As I looked,

"thrones were set in place,
    and the Ancient of Days took his seat.
His clothing was as white as snow;
    the hair of his head was white like wool.
His throne was flaming with fire,
    and its wheels were all ablaze.
A river of fire was flowing,
    coming out from before him.
Thousands upon thousands attended him;
    ten thousand times ten thousand stood before him.
The court was seated,
    and the books were opened." (Dan 7:9-10 NIV)

Yahweh is presented as holy, ineffable, eternal and all-powerful. All the empires of the world are impotent before this king and judge. It is this king and judge who cries out like a woman in labor, giving birth to our redemption and restoration. Only this one—the Ancient of Days—can change our world, and those of us who have heard God's groans and responded in faith are invited to serve God in this empire-shattering work.

Our hope throughout this book is to explore what this might look like in real terms today. To do this, we don't only want to detail steps and stages and practical applications. We want to redesign the very metaphors the church has been using to understand its role in the world. But before we get there we need to look closely at the current assumptions and practices of the church that are standing in our way.

2

WHAT'S STANDING IN OUR WAY?

There should be a difference in the community because the church exists, and if it left for some reason, there should be a void that's felt. Unfortunately, that's not often the case. We become more about church preservation than community transformation.

ED STETZER

In this clash of empires that Daniel dreams of, how can a "more relevant" church be the full answer? We are not suggesting that culture-shaping doesn't include church growth or legislation. We just think those are too limited. And we think the evidence from the past fifty years bears that out. While some conservative Christians have been outraged by the claims of people like columnist Cal Thomas saying that Christian political engagement has achieved little since the 1970s, that doesn't mean Christians should retreat from the political process. Christians should indeed engage these issues deeply. In fact, we believe Christians can be, should be and indeed are present in every aspect of society, bringing God's perspective on *all* of life that is shaped by Jesus, not merely reducing the Christian mandate to what some pundits call "front-burner moral concerns" (discrediting the theory of evolution, defending traditional marriage and opposing abortion).

Likewise, while we don't put all our hope in church growth and church planting, we love church planters. We love their heart for people, their enthusiasm and their never-say-die attitude to any challenging circumstance. We agree that the world needs more churches. But we aren't convinced that more and better churches should ever be the sole objective. Planting more churches isn't a silver bullet. Seeing church planting as part of a greater vision for the birth of a new world seems reasonable to us, but not as an end in itself. Perhaps planting new churches and the growth of existing churches is more of a fruit of God's vision than a goal to chase after.

So, what's standing in our way? Why has there been so little overall impact for all our effort (significant as it is) in church growth strategies and political engagement? We suggest the following reasons.

THE DOMINANCE OF SUNDAY

Clearly, if the church is to have meaningful cultural effect it must be engaged at every aspect of society. This is why we don't rule out political activity at all. We think Christians should be affecting the way the country does politics, business, the legal process, education, the arts and more. To quote N. T. Wright again,

> We are called to be *part of* God's new creation, called to be *agents of* that new creation here and now. We are called to *model and display* that new creation in symphonies and family life, in restorative justice and poetry, in holiness and service to the poor, in politics and painting.[1]

In our vision of birthing a new world, as in Wright's, if agents of that new world flooded every aspect of society and brought their values informed by Christ to bear, we could see a serious altering of the path our culture is taking. This has to include a recognition of the contribution of all Christians to culture-shaping in every aspect of society. It is not merely about changing the church, but changing the whole world. Wright explains this further:

> The world of space, time, and matter is where real people live, where real communities happen, where difficult decisions are taken, where schools and hospitals bear witness to the "now, already" of the gospel while police and prisons bear witness to the "not yet." The world of space, time, and matter is where parliaments, city councils, neighborhood watch groups, and everything in between are set up and run for the benefit of the wider community, the community where anarchy means that bullies (economic and social as well as physical) will always win, where the weak and vulnerable will always need protecting, and where therefore the social and political structures of society are part of the Creator's design. And the church that is renewed by the message of Jesus's resurrection must be the church that goes to work precisely in that space, time, and matter and that claims it in advance as the place of God's kingdom, of Jesus's lordship, of the power of the Spirit.[2]

This space, time and matter to which Dr. Wright refers must necessarily include our Monday-to-Friday lives. Christians need to be equipped to be agents of change in their vocations for the sake of Christ.

Recently, I (Michael) met a Christian man named Ed who has been working in the California education system, seeking to revive flagging local schools in poor neighborhoods. A gifted leader with a PhD in educational administration, he has worked his way up the bureaucratic system and might have contented himself with a comfortable government job with a corner office. Instead, he chose to take a demotion and work as a district superintendent in a socially and economically deprived town. His most recent challenge has been to revitalize three underperforming high schools. Ed believes that reviving schools leads to neighborhoods that flourish. And it's working. When I asked him what support or help his own church or other local churches had given him, he looked at me blankly. It hadn't occurred to him that church might have had any contribution to make to this endeavor. But surely Ed's empire-shattering work is the work God calls us to in this broken world. It challenges the beasts of privilege, poverty and entrenched disadvantage. We suggest that such incredibly useful work gets overlooked, not because we think helping whole neighborhoods to flourish isn't kingdom work, but because it's not the kind of work that pastors usually participate in or support.

A significant way the church joins God in birthing the new creation is to unleash, shape, nurture and support people like Ed to do what God has called them to. Whether the new creation is modeled and displayed in music, poetry or painting, family life, restorative justice or service to the poor, it must operate in realms beyond which the clergy normally engage.

There is often a narrative in our churches that states that no matter your income base, the time, talent and treasure you possess are most valuable in the church in order to run and fund church programs and pay the clergy, all to fuel the ministries employed by the church to bless the city. As for evangelism and disciple-making, your good and moral example, your ability to articulate your own testimony, and your loving disposition where you work, play or live is meant to attract people to the gospel and ultimately lead them to join the church, or more specifically, to join *your* church.

Each of us has an ultimate contribution in life, and that is much more than simply supporting and funding church programs to increase church attendance. We are uniquely called to join God's redemptive plan to improve the world, not simply to improve the church. Our churches have the opportunity to resource and equip their congregants to discern their calling and to make vocational decisions, viewing their careers and everyday life as sacred places where God is at work.

Justin Vandewater in Sioux Falls, South Dakota, found himself at a crossroads after years of serving in the local church. With a conviction that all of us, no matter our life work, have a primary calling to join the mission of God to love the world, he cocreated a ministry called Our Primary, which comes alongside Jesus followers to help them discover their primary calling expressed in every sector of life. Through workshops and one-on-one coaching, Justin and team are awakening people to their dreams and helping them view their vocation as a valuable aspect of God's mission. We aren't implying that followers of Jesus shouldn't view their service and volunteer work in church activities as valuable. Rather, we're saying their contribution to culture-shaping shouldn't be limited to those things.

Jesus followers are in fact engaged in a variety of sectors of society and doing remarkable things to stimulate culture-altering change. Unfortunately, many churches have undervalued or undersupported their congregants in living out their God-given calling in their places of passion, profession and creativity. Churches are filled with gifted individuals who crave companions, mentors, mothers and fathers to walk beside them on the journey of life with Jesus and to help them discover the ways they can join God's renewal in the world.

Investing deeply in the lives of church members won't happen at any given Sunday gathering. These kinds of investments require committed, life-on-life relationships. We fear that many people are leaving the church because of a lack of relational connectedness that can support and fan the flame of their dreams and callings.

The term "dechurched" is sometimes used to describe those who were once part of an organized church expression but have left for one reason or another. Just because they left the institution of church, however, doesn't mean they don't maintain an enduring love for Jesus. One such leader in particular comes to mind. Emilie worked at a large church for over twelve years. Eager to love people and foster Bible-centered community, she finished her Master of Divinity degree and joined the pastoral staff. Emilie taught, discipled, organized volunteers and completed any odd job necessary to help the church run as smoothly as possible. A few years in, Emilie, then in her early thirties, had a growing heart for contemplative spirituality and a fuller participation in what God was doing outside the walls of her very successful church. She sensed it was time to branch out and start another church expression, one that God had been formulating in her imagination for some time. Stepping away from a big church was heart wrenching and liberating all at the same time. She knew God was leading her out, but her vision was misunderstood and unsupported by her fellow staff members. The uncertainty of the future was heavy on her heart, yet she, like many others, took the risk to step forward in following God.

Sadly, some clergy epitomize people like Emilie merely as "church leavers." We're growing tired of reading blogs and articles about why millennials are leaving the church that seek to blame people like Emilie for a lack of commitment or a poor ecclesiology. Many are leaving because they believe the vocation of following Christ and changing the world can't be contained to ecclesial or Sunday-based work. Many of them are simply obeying God's guidance to create something other than what they've seen. These so-called dechurched people could be on the cusp of the church of the future. They are searching for meaning, purpose and a community to belong to that will help them wrestle with life questions, support them in everyday life puzzles and compel them to faithfully live, love and lead as followers of Jesus. One of the most common sentiments expressed by those who've left the institutional church is that the act of *going* to church had minimal impact on their daily life, even though, again, Jesus still impacts them greatly. Some would go further to say that they actually *found* Jesus when they chose to break away from the institutionalized Jesus they experienced in their church expression.

Leaving the institution of church as they know it has compelled people to create community in other ways—community composed through service projects, activism, contemplation, substance abuse support groups, creative placemaking endeavors, justice projects, discussion podcasts, recreational hobbies, work/entrepreneurial ventures, health and wellness groups, neighborhood groups, life-stage affinity groups, etc. In these forms of community, people are pursuing the meaning of life with a deep longing for connectedness, inner peace and a sense that they are making a difference in the world. Our concern is to ask why they had to leave the church to find this. Can't people discover this sense of mission *through* the church rather than by leaving it? Can't clergy and fellow church members foster their mission and hold them in love and accountability? Or are these signs of the birth of the church in places we often overlook, outside our typical church paradigm? What is Christ doing here?

If we want to enter more bountifully into the story of God in our neighborhoods and cities, we must move beyond only the Sunday experience and learn to accept ourselves as a part of a wider community. When we hear pastors bemoaning the decline of their congregations we think they may need to be released to pastor their neighborhoods. Measuring success solely on the numbers in the pews can be soul destroying for many church leaders. Yet the people outside the walls of our churches, whether unchurched or dechurched, are aching for honest souls and competent pastors who will come alongside them, shepherd them and help them find God in the midst of their communities. By limiting the work of discipleship in the ways we've described, pastors run the risk of limiting the culture-shaping work to which we're all called.

COLONIZING METHODOLOGIES

A second reason why the church often has little impact in altering culture is its predilection for top-down approaches to bringing change. The planning of "campaigns" to bring change has often appeared as an attempt to lord it over others, to try to legislate morality, or to insist on the socially privileged position of the church (even if that was never the intention). We agree with Lesslie Newbigin, who insisted that the church needs to recover an eschatology that recognizes that our political or religious activity cannot establish the kingdom of God. That is God's work, and God is leading history to its ultimate end. When the church seeks to exercise a power differential from the state and seeks to impose its views on others it only creates resentment and suspicion.

This "colonizing" impulse can be seen when churches exist in one location and plant ministries in the underprivileged neighborhoods in another. Often these ministries are a blessing to the people they serve in the poorer areas of town but they remain at service provision status, never actually accompanying local residents to invest in their own development and the betterment of their own context. Despite their provision of needed services, the approach of such churches can feed a cycle of poverty and oppression instead of addressing the greater needs. We're not questioning the good motives of the churches that do this, just the unintended consequences of the action.

Amber and Matthew Ayers have another vision we find to be quite compelling. Amber is an ECO Presbyterian pastor in Colorado Springs, and her husband, Matthew, is the executive director of Dream Centers locally. In response to this colonizing tendency of the white American church, they sensed God inviting them to buy a home in an ethnically diverse, underresourced neighborhood and live there with a small community of Jesus followers. They are moving in as listeners and learners, committed to the long, laborious and joy-filled path of trusting what God will birth in their place, in God's way and at God's pace. Amber also has a vocational call to train and equip leaders within her context. But the Ayerses are committed to patiently waiting on the Spirit, and rather than going in to start a ministry in the neighborhood or launching a church plant, this couple is stepping into the unknown with an ever deepening hope in God's goodness and the fact that, like a birthing mother, God is bringing life there.

The alternative (and sadly more common) approach would be for a couple like the Ayerses, or a small group like theirs, to move in and act like an expert on what their new neighbors need. When such a group moves in with prefabricated ministry plans and imposes those plans on their neighbors without listening, without consultation or collaboration, they come off like they know best. They adopt a top-down approach, as though they have the answers to their new neighbors' problems and they have arrived to fix them.

In a provocatively titled blog post, "Urban Church ~~Planting~~ Plantations," Christena Cleveland highlights the corrosive social impact of white suburban Christians flooding into urban communities, intending to serve Christ there but actually contributing to an unhealthy gentrification of such neighborhoods. She wrote, "I've seen predominantly white, wealthy suburban churches take an imperialistic glance at the urban center, decide that they are called to 'take back the city' and then proceed with all of the honor and finesse of a military invasion."[3] Instead of birthing the redemptive possibilities in the city in keeping with the values of the reign of God, these colonizing churches have inadvertently contributed to inequity, differentiation and separation. Cleveland speaks directly to the us-and-them ideology, specifically relating to the ministry strategies employed by churches of privilege, imposing their way of doing church in contexts that they consider to be "high need." She says,

> If we truly saw ourselves as an interdependent body with a shared Head, resources, blood, and life, then suburban churches that want to love on a city wouldn't do it by expanding their empires across city lines. They would do it by truly sharing their resources, blood and life in service to the Head. . . . The empire says that *our* church needs to be present in every community, *our* church has the answers, and *our* church's resources are our resources alone. If we follow this path, power dynamics remain unchanged and urban church plantations ensue.[4]

Whether a monocultural church of privilege entering into a more diverse, inner-city setting or a church planter moving into a context where she or he is among peers, the us-and-them mentality of churches is a dominant barrier to participating in birthing the redeeming work of God. Such change occurs when we enter—truly enter—our neighborhoods and partner with our neighbors, rather than imposing our externally created strategies.

ROOTLESS CHURCHES

A third concern we have for why the church seems to have less and less effect in altering culture is the development of "rootless church" models. Whereas "colonizing" churches do physically move into a community but have the tendency to dominate their neighbors, rootless churches are characterized by the absence of any members even living in the neighborhood. These are either churches whose members have all moved away from the neighborhood but who continue to commute to the church on Sundays, or externally imposed new churches that are parachuted into a neighborhood rather than growing up in the soil in which they're planted.

It is interesting to us that while the language of "planting" has become more popular, the idea of "roots" has become less so. These nonindigenous churches are portable and foreign, and are often perceived as being inflicted upon a community rather than emerging organically. Their relational connection to their neighbors is flimsy. And the social projects they undertake often feel imposed. We shudder when we hear people advising rootless churches to "pick a missional project" in their community to get involved with, as though mission is a smorgasbord or buffet, rather than a relationship and a vocation.

I (Christiana) had an encounter with a church group having a picnic in my neighborhood park in San Diego one holiday afternoon. I learned that this group was a "gospel centered Christian church plant" that meets on Sundays in a school auditorium about twenty minutes away from our park. Depending on the growth of their weekly service attendance, this church wasn't sure how long they would be able to stay in their current location. According to their website, the church has an admirable and loving heart for the city of San Diego. They want to plant ten churches in the next five years, churches that "help people find restoration in God." I noticed, however, that there was not one mention of a commitment to neighborhood or a focused geographical place in any of their statements of mission, purpose or belief. And they came to hang out in our park because, well, they don't have a park of their own. This is basically what we'd call a rootless church.

This church gathering meets in a school building that is located in a particular neighborhood primarily because that's where the church leadership found the most affordable space to rent, conducive to their needs. They have a regional vision for ministering to the city but their neighborhood vision is limited. At any given moment they can metaphorically lift up their church and transport it to any other neighborhood that would better fit their growing needs for more space to host larger gatherings of people. At the new location, not much would change. They would have to reorient to their new spatial layout and figure out how to set up their new staging for weekend services, but other than those minor inconveniences, everything else would pretty much stay the same. And who knows, maybe the neighborhood they left behind wouldn't even notice their absence, except for less of a parking nightmare on Sundays.

This is an increasingly common expression of church today. I (Michael) recently met an architect in Los Angeles who had designed a lot of megachurch campuses. One of the obstacles he had to overcome when building a new church facility was that the neighbors think of such buildings as a LULU. In architect-speak that's "locally undesirable land use." In other words, if there's a vacant tract of land in your area, one of its least desirable uses, as far as the neighbors are concerned, is a church. New churches aren't usually beautiful buildings. They are considered unusable by the general community. And they bring outsiders to the neighborhood every Sunday, clogging the streets and disturbing the amenity of the place. We're not saying larger congregations don't need appropriately large facilities in which to meet, but when the members of those congregations don't live in the neighborhood, their buildings are sadly designated as LULUs.

We are concerned that as Western Christians our lack of commitment to a people and a place and our penchant for portability has cut us off at the roots. This also translates into the way in which we refuse to inhabit the neighborhoods where we live. Without roots, we slowly die, bearing no good fruit. And the fruit we long for is the culture-altering transformation in the redemptive plan of God.

In their book *The New Parish*, our good friends Paul Sparks, Tim Soerens and Dwight Friesen articulate an alternative reality for the people of God, reintegrating our practices of community, formation and mission embedded in localized expressions. It is in the integration of these practices that we are faithfully present in everyday realities to experience the movement of the Spirit of God in, among and through us in transformational ways. They write,

> When local followers of Christ engage in this process of reintegration, we find support for reconciling our whole lives within the limitations of a faith community rooted in a specific time and place. When this happens the love of God manifests itself in holistic love of neighbor.[5]

As we reintegrate our lives in neighborhoods, towns and villages we begin to notice that God is inviting us to be faithfully present in places where God is already birthing kingdom realities. Churches are finding that very few of their members live in the neighborhood where the church is situated. These churches are made up of folks who commute in once or twice a week for a church event of some kind. They support international missionaries, mission organizations and citywide outreach initiatives, but they have little to no engagement in the daily struggles of the very neighborhood where their church building sits. The rootlessness of the church affects the neighborhood. In a conversation with two of my (Christiana's) neighbors, I inquired about the influence that local churches have had over the past few decades, specifically within our shared neighborhood context. This couple, who would categorize themselves as atheist spirituals, has lived in my neighborhood of Golden Hill for fifty-nine years. In all the years spent raising their children and participating in the life of the neighborhood, they could only name one church (of the seven churches that have existed in the neighborhood for more than twenty years each) that they've seen to have any kind of influence for good in the place they call home. The particular church they referred to hosts a monthly food bank, serving the impoverished from the downtown San Diego area. It is not that churches aren't doing good and noteworthy activities, it's that the vision of the church is too small and often without roots. Never underestimate how much our neighborhoods notice our lack of care.

JESUS, MOTHERS, WARRIORS, FURY

Returning to Daniel's dream in Daniel 7, the evil empires of his world are not only shattered by the Ancient of Days, but through the clouds and flame of the celestial throne room Daniel sees a mysterious figure. He looks like a man, or a "son of man," and to him all dominion and authority is granted. We know the identity of that mysterious figure. Jesus self-consciously appropriates the language of Daniel 7 and applies it to himself. At his trial before the high priest, Jesus is asked whether he is the Messiah. He replies, "You have said so. . . . But I say to all of you: From now on you will see the Son of Man sitting at the right hand of the Mighty One and coming on the clouds of heaven" (Mt 26:64 NIV).

We believe that Jesus is the hope of nations and that God is birthing a new world right here in the midst of the broken one. Jesus' own death on the cross mirrors the pain and anguish of childbirth. Indeed, it is through his death that Jesus gives birth to the new covenant for all who believe. Jesus' silent, uncomplaining death mirrors God's seeming silence during the Babylonian exile generations before. And the scoffers mocked him for his weakness. "You who are going to destroy the temple and build it in three days, save yourself! Come down from the cross, if you are the Son of God!" (Mt 27:40 NIV). But as we know, Jesus' humble death wasn't an act of frailty. It was a supreme work of power. Jesus was giving birth.

If we return to the words of Isaiah 42 where we began, it is important to note the context of the reference to Yahweh groaning as a birthing mother in verse 14. The previous verse describes God as a (male?) warrior:

> The LORD goes forth like a soldier,
>> like a warrior he stirs up his fury;
> he cries out, he shouts aloud,
>> he shows himself mighty against his foes. (Is 42:13)

And in the following verse, Isaiah hears God declare:

> I will lay waste mountains and hills,
>> and dry up all their herbage;
> I will turn the rivers into islands,
>> and dry up the pools. (Is 42:15)

So the reference to the vulnerable birthing woman is set between two images of power and fury. Jesus was mute before his accusers, but in no way should this imply weakness. At first the idea of juxtaposing warriors with mothers, and birthing with destruction, seems odd. But for those who have given birth (as Christiana has), or who have stood helplessly alongside their wife during childbirth (as Michael has), or for anyone who bears the scars of self-sacrifice for the sake of others, the idea of fury and rage doesn't seem so out of place. Verses 13 and 15 need to be read when we think of God panting as a birthing mother. The terror, the gasps, the anguish you are seeing, says God, are the birth pangs of something new, to which I am giving birth! And the church is invited to assist in its delivery, as we will explain in subsequent chapters.

3 A DIVINE DISRUPTION

No obstacle is so big that one person with determination can't make a difference.

JAY SAMIT

J esus described the world that God is giving birth to as "the kingdom of God," and his parables reveal his conviction that this world begins small, like a newborn baby, but grows in size and influence inexorably throughout history.

In Matthew 13, he describes it as a seed, pregnant with life, planted in rich soil that reproduces a hundred, sixty or thirty times what was sown (v. 8). Later he compares it to a mustard seed, saying that even though the seed is tiny it produces one of largest and most unruly of trees (vv. 31-32). In the same chapter, Jesus describes the kingdom of God as yeast (v. 33), a treasure buried in a field, and a string of pearls worth a merchant's whole fortune (vv. 44-46).

In every case he describes something small that grows and yields great influence and accrues great value. Jesus was planting the seeds of this world, knowing they would take root and flourish into a world-changing force—a huge, boisterous, dynamic movement that would grow and grow around the world and throughout history. Indeed, God's own incarnation is a physical enactment of this movement. Born fragile and tiny in a stable in Bethlehem, the Messiah grew in stature and unleashed a movement through which he shook Rome to its core.

Mary knew, as she awaited the birth of the Messiah Jesus, that in her womb she carried the one who was to interrupt human progress like no other. Myriad prophecies like the one in Daniel 7 we explored earlier spoke about the child growing inside her. Mary yearned for a Messiah who would tear down the oppressive regime and establish a new kingdom of justice.

The incarnation was a severe disruption of an existing paradigm. God chose to enter the world through the womb of a virgin Jewish peasant girl from the small village of Nazareth. Mary faced an uncertain future with potential retribution from her whole community. The Gospel of Matthew is careful to state that Joseph, her fiancé, planned to quietly release her from her commitment to marry him rather than expose her to public humiliation and torture (Mt 1:18-19). According to Jewish law, this young girl could have been stoned to death as a punishment for adultery had she been found out.

So Mary courageously accepts the call and carries the Christ child to full term, anticipating an alteration of life as she knew it. What a bold, venturesome and heroic young woman! Jesus the baby boy would stir up the family system into which he was born. There would be dissonance, reorientation and adjustment for Mary's new family. Jesus the Messiah, God in flesh, would disrupt the social order into which he was born. The political stasis would be rattled, power structures confronted, injustices brought to light and a strong voice given to the weak. In the turbulent waiting Mary sang, holding together the grittiness of her own life on the margins and a resilient hope in the God she trusted. Mary proclaimed the identity of Jesus as Messiah in what we've come to know as the Magnificat.

In its Latin translation, *Magnificat* is the first word of a longer phrase, *Magnificat anima mea Dominum,* translated, "My soul magnifies the Lord":

> And Mary said,
> "My soul magnifies the Lord,
>   and my spirit rejoices in God my Savior,
> for he has looked with favor on the lowliness of his servant.
>   Surely, from now on all generations will call me blessed;
> for the Mighty One has done great things for me,
>   and holy is his name.
> His mercy is for those who fear him
>   from generation to generation.
> He has shown strength with his arm;
>   he has scattered the proud in the thoughts of their hearts.
> He has brought down the powerful from their thrones,
>   and lifted up the lowly;
> he has filled the hungry with good things,
>   and sent the rich away empty.
> He has helped his servant Israel,
>   in remembrance of his mercy,
> according to the promise he made to our ancestors,
>   to Abraham and to his descendants forever."
> (Lk 1:46-55)

Mary laments her own pain and that of the weary world around her. Her faith is fierce. Carolyn Sharp says she envisions Mary as "a girl who sings defiantly to her God through her tears, fists clenched against an unknown future. Mary's courageous song of praise is a radical resource for those seeking to honor the holy amid the suffering and conflicts of real life."[1]

In the 1980s, the Guatemalan government decided that Mary's words about God's preferential love for the poor were too dangerous and revolutionary. The words of the Magnificat had been stirring the hearts of Guatamala's poor population. Mary's words about the Christ child were inspiring the poor to believe that freedom and change were indeed possible and that following the way of Jesus would interrupt the flow of civilization as they knew it. As passion swelled, the government banned any public recitation of the Magnificat. Likewise, in Argentina, the Mothers of the Plaza de Mayo, whose husbands and children had been disappeared under the country's oppressive military dictatorship, posted copies of the Magnificat throughout the central plaza of the capital to protest this injustice. These women were initial responders as lives were taken and families were broken apart by Argentina's military regime. Their activism not only helped rescue lives but also created local and global awareness around issues of human rights violations in Latin America and elsewhere.

Jesus turns everything upside down, pulling apart kingdoms and announcing the full reign of God in his words, in his deeds and in the power of the Spirit. The incarnation disrupts the fabric of society and changes history forever.

German theologian Dietrich Bonheoffer reflected on the revolutionary nature of Mary's song in an Advent sermon he gave in 1933. He said,

> The song of Mary is the oldest Advent hymn. It is at once the most passionate, the wildest, one might even say the most revolutionary Advent hymns ever sung. This is not the gentle, tender, dreamy Mary whom we sometimes see in paintings; this is the passionate, surrendered, proud, enthusiastic Mary who speaks out here. This song . . . is a hard, strong, inexorable

song about collapsing thrones and humbled lords of this world, about the power of God and the powerlessness of humankind. These are the tones of the women prophets of the Old Testament that now come to life in Mary's mouth.[2]

The provocative message in the song of Mary continues to disrupt our world today. If we believe Mary's words to be true, then there is great hope for the ongoing redemption of God, especially in the darkest corners of our world. A new world was being birthed and continues to be birthed to this day. And perhaps Mary's words communicate the call and the purpose of the community of faith that chooses to align with this mission of God in Jesus. Certainly, following this way of life is revolutionary. When the followers of the Incarnate One enter into a neighborhood or a group or a community, they cannot help but create disruption because they come as representatives of the Disruptive One. But more than that, the church has to remain conscious of the fact that God is birthing a new world in Christ. God is scattering the proud, bringing down rulers from their thrones, lifting up the humble and feeding the hungry with good things. As this world unfurls around us, we join as partners in God's restorative purposes.

Like families, all networks—whether subcultures, religious communities or whole neighborhoods—function with some form of existing balance. The introduction of a new element—a new baby, a different religious affiliation, another person or a community that is devoted to living out the values of Christ in the world—will always upset that balance. We repeat: it will *always* upset that balance. The question we need to face is not, Is God changing things here? but, *In what ways* am I willing to participate in those changes?

All environments strive for equilibrium. It's also called *stasis*, from the Greek for "a standing still." This is a state of stability in which all forces are equal and opposing, thereby balancing each other out. Our bodies do it. Our families do it. Whole societies do it. When a source of disequilibrium is introduced, our desire for stasis means we either assimilate the newly introduced agent or expel it. In fact, stasis knows only the adaptation or expulsion of a newly introduced element. Following Jesus, among other things, necessarily requires that to some degree we must see ourselves as a source of disequilibrium in an environment yearning for stasis. Avoiding expulsion would seem obvious, but what does the alternative—assimilation—look like for those of us who desire to incarnate the goodness of Jesus in our contexts? How can we think about adaptation into a neighborhood or community in a way that doesn't cause us to be so molded by our environment that our presence brings nothing to it? In brief, those committed to the incarnational way of Jesus are seeking to alter the environment in which they live life. And the environment doesn't want to be altered.

Some of us misread this resistance to change. Some see it as persecution for their faith or defiance to the things of God. Sometimes those things are present, but often the opposition that the incarnational church experiences is the normal effect of stasis. When we're not aware of this, we tend toward either separation or compromise. We either separate ourselves from those who don't believe what we believe or we compromise our identity altogether. Both approaches are calamitous. The invitation of God is to incarnate in the way of Jesus, living wholeheartedly in the world as we are transformed by the presence of the Holy Spirit in the places where we live, work, serve and play. It is the Spirit within us that impacts and alters the environments we inhabit. It is the same Spirit in us and all around us that impacts and alters us.

Following God into the old world and participating in the birthing of the new creation is the very work of God's people. As God gives birth to this new world, we are invited, like midwives, to attend and assist in the delivery.

PURSUING GOD'S RESTORATIVE PURPOSES

Much has been written about missional living that emphasizes neighborliness, hospitality, justice-seeking and the like. There has been a reasonable concern about not wanting to cause offense to our communities, to gain the trust of our neighbors, to counteract the stereotypes of obnoxious Christianity and its condemnation of everything secular. Before we know it, we run the risk of compromising our deepest identity in Christ that compels us to live for a dream that includes but goes beyond community gardens and neighborhood improvement. The message of Jesus brings offense. It doesn't leave us or our surrounding environments unaltered. And those filled with the gospel and impelled to offer it as a gift in new places become a presence that disturbs their neighbors. Our call and our hope is to allow the gospel to disturb people for good, Christ-filled reasons as agents of transformational change at a soul level, affecting the very fabric of society.

If we are to be change agents, then what is the change we want to see? Surely it results in a change of heart among our neighbors. And yet, if we adopt a compromising stance we will find that it is possible to engage in neighborliness and community development without ever making such an impact at a heart level. Could it be that our social clubs, meet-up groups, community gardens and even our justice-seeking forums run the risk of being, at their core, heartless? To be seen merely as being a good neighbor isn't enough. We're reminded of the Anglican bishop who once said, "Everywhere Paul went he caused a riot. Everywhere I go they make me a cup of tea." But we would like to suggest that principled, ethical, incarnational life will reside somewhere between a riot and a cup of tea— that is, between separation and compromise.

God is birthing new realities, and they necessarily bring changes. By this we don't mean that the Christian message can be reduced to something like, "I love you. Now change." That kind of approach has led to great resentment by many people, who hear Christians setting themselves up as somehow superior to everyone else. Change begins with simple, authentic and everyday acts of great love. We see our mutual need to enter an ongoing process of being altered by God to conform to God's pattern for humankind. Like Paul David Tripp's description of us, we are "people in need of change helping people in need of change."[3] We must explore the importance of principled, relational mission, while also addressing the need for ethical and intentional models of incarnational presence that bring about God-honoring change to individuals and whole societies. And all the while we must never forget that our churches are not the solution to the world's problems but a sign that another way—God's way—is possible.

James Davison Hunter refers to our incarnational calling as "faithful presence." In his book *To Change the World,* he explores the idea that when Christians practice faithful presence, by making disciples and serving the common good, they will alter the world around them, not because they set out to do so, but because disciple-making and service shift the delicate cultural balance. He says, "If there are benevolent consequences of our engagement with the world . . . it is precisely because it is *not* rooted in a desire to change the world for the better but rather because it is an expression of a desire to honor the creator of all goodness, beauty, and truth, a manifestation of our loving obedience to God, and a fulfillment of God's command to love our neighbor."[4]

Honoring the creator, loving our neighbors, serving the common good and standing up for what is good and just—these very actions cannot help but bring a new element into an existing system. They upset the stasis, and it is not always appreciated; it is usually resisted stridently. The powerful resist change because their position depends on the status quo. The disempowered often resist change too, not because they enjoy the status quo, but because they have acquiesced to it. But simply because it might cause a riot isn't reason enough for us to withdraw. Again, as Hunter says, "To be Christian is to be obliged to engage the world, pursuing God's restorative purposes over all of life."[5] We need to be aware of the challenges we face when we seek to engage the world to which we've been sent.

WE ALTER ANY SYSTEM WE TRULY ENTER

One of the key understandings we need to adopt is that we cannot help but alter any system we genuinely enter. Those churches that have no effect on their neighborhoods have clearly never entered them (i.e., they are rootless). But if we do choose to meaningfully engage the existing systems around us, we will necessarily change them.

Let us give you a simple example. In the 1970s therapist Murray Bowen developed "family systems theory," asserting that every family is a system that craves stasis. Every member is interconnected, and each member, through a myriad of unspoken cues, develops a clear sense of the role they have to play in the family system. Bowen famously said, "On one level each family member is an individual, but on a deeper level the central family group is as one."[6]

Within that family oneness, each member comes to act in predictable ways, based on the role they play and the roles other family members play. As long as they all play their roles and maintain the "rules" there is balance in the system. Movement of one affects all the others.

For example, if a mother drifts into alcoholism, the whole family system adapts to manage that fact. Her unpredictability, violence, contempt and self-focus distort much of the family's interaction. So, the whole family does things such as absorbing the anger, denying the effect of the alcoholic's behavior, avoiding her and even trying to cover up the disease. And each member of the family often plays a slightly different role in managing the behavior. That role-playing then develops patterns of interaction that become ingrained habits, making change extremely difficult. And every family has certain rules that are self-regulating and peculiar to itself. The family is a purposeful system; it has a goal, and usually the goal is to remain intact as a family. That's why family systems therapists believe real healing can never fully occur if only one member of a family is seeking treatment.

Often the strength of a family system isn't felt until a new element is introduced. When the eldest daughter gets married, her new husband might question why everyone is covering up for his mother-in-law's alcoholism, causing considerable family angst. As a newly introduced element to the system his presence has a bump-on effect to everyone else in that system. You see, as burdensome as it might be to have a close family member suffering from alcoholism, the system works by accommodating that family member, no matter how dysfunctional things become. While family systems are resistant to dramatic change, they make constant small shifts and adjustments to accommodate and respond to its members and changes in its environment.

Now consider the scenario wherein one member of a family has a radical conversion to Christ. When that family member tries to bring his or her brand of faith into the family there is often an upheaval in the system. Christians often interpret this naively as a form of persecution, or the work of Satan, but very often it's simply a family's response to disequilibrium in the system. The family system has developed stasis around that family member being a particular person and behaving in a particular manner. The transformation in values, beliefs and behaviors that occurs when someone becomes a Christian means that person no longer plays the same role in that system. Even if the change that occurs in the new believer is for the better (as you'd hope), the system is used to operating in a particular way.

This isn't to suggest that systemic change isn't possible. Indeed, it's the very hope of Christian mission. We are seeking to be used by God to bring about individual and communal change, to see people set free from fear and sin and death, and to invite them to participate in the repair of human society, the breaking in of God's reign here on earth. Altering things is God's business.

In families, change occurs for two broad reasons. First, there are normative changes that occur. Naturally, as the family grows and changes through time, expected changes occur. Little kids become teenagers. Teenagers leave home to go to school. Parents experience midlife issues. These changes affect the way the family interacts. But these changes are generally gradual and predictable (although sometimes no less difficult). But second, changes in a family system can be caused by non-normative stresses or crises—sudden unemployment or critical illness, the introduction of a new family member or the loss of an existing one.

Change and the process of birth is an experience not to be inhibited. Just as there is gradual growth and change in any social system, we mustn't forget that there are almost ten months of gestation before new life emerges into the world. And those months of waiting and growth are often filled with a blend of excitement, fear and uncertainty. In the process of change, of course, gradual, manageable and predictable growth is always more desirable, but we all know that people can experience enormous personal growth through tragedies like failure, crisis, illness and grief. If we desire to participate in altering the system into which we've entered, we should aim to do so with authenticity, gradually moving through necessary steps and following along already established relational and social channels. And sometimes God chooses to change things very quickly!

If you look at this in terms of whole neighborhoods, you'll see it operates similarly to a family system. Neighborhoods desire stasis too. It's obvious that massive changes occur when a big box store moves into town. But there are knock-on effects whenever any commercial change happens in a community. When a new business is introduced, new neighbors move in, tragedy hits in a business or household, or someone joins the neighborhood council with a specific agenda, these dynamics create disequilibrium. My (Christiana's) local grocery store recently changed owners, transforming a run-of-the-mill shopping spot, geared predominantly toward the Latino population, to a trendy hipster shop selling microbrew and overpriced organic quinoa. Ironically, the grocery store is sandwiched between a low-cost Latino hair salon and a popular Mexican bakery called Panchitas. These significant changes have caused an interesting tension within the neighborhood itself. Parts of the neighborhood are adapting well to the change, grateful for the aesthetic upgrades, for the fact that the employees of the previous store were able keep their jobs and for the expanded alcohol selection. But the recipients of WIC (a subsidized food program for women, infants and children) can no longer purchase most of the food there and took the brunt. And of course, the customer demographic is shifting. It is hard to say whether this is a move of progress or regression. But the simple change of one grocery store is ricocheting around the neighborhood in a classic case of social disequilibrium.

How we insert ourselves into a context, how we practice incarnation —how we introduce ourselves to an environment, how we partner with our neighbors, how we read our neighborhood—is important. You will alter your environment. The question is, In which ways are you willing to do so?

I (Michael) remember being at an outdoor market full of farm-fresh produce, vintage finds and homespun arts and crafts, when I approached a table selling colorful stones and crystals. The vendor looked very gothic in her hooded purple shrug with lace sleeves, festooned with symbolic pagan jewelry. She was engaged in an animated conversation with a potential customer about the therapeutic qualities of certain crystals. As I approached her table, she stopped suddenly in midsentence and turned toward me. "Are you a Christian?" she asked abruptly. I acknowledged that I was, and she nodded sagely. "I thought so," she said. "You just caused a whole lot of interference in my senses."

A whole lot of interference in my senses. We like that. Clearly this woman was pretty tapped in to the spiritual realm, and the presence of the Holy Spirit within Michael created static for her. Most people you meet in your neighborhood won't be as spiritually attuned, but in a very real sense your presence (or the presence of God in you) will cause static. You'll create interference, hopefully in a good and intriguing way, rather than in an annoying and offensive manner. Later we'll explore frameworks for getting that balance right.

A SLIGHT DEVIATION FROM EXPECTATION

Sometimes, we imagine that the disruption we've been called to initiate has to be something cataclysmic. But that's not necessarily so. As the birth of a tiny baby can bring huge changes, the introduction of just a small new element can create a big long-term ripple. In art appreciation there's a thing called Berlyne's Law, named after a psychologist who sought to employ the tools of his discipline to an understanding of how art influences emotion. It basically goes like this: what strikes us as good art is usually a slight deviation from our expectations. Art that deviates too much from our expectations is alienating and bizarre. That's why many of us struggle in galleries of contemporary art. Highly abstract and experimental art throws us off balance. We just don't *get* it. But alternatively, according to Berlyne, if a piece of art conforms too perfectly to our expectations it is considered boring. A dull but perfectly executed landscape is easily overlooked. The types of images that grab our attention deviate from convention, *but not too much*. As Neal Roese says, "Somewhere in between the extremes of the boring and the bizarre lays a sweet zone of recognition coupled with mild surprise."[7] And it's that mild surprise that makes all the difference. Missional living in contemporary secular society requires a deft ability to land between the boring and the bizarre.

We can all think of examples of the socially bizarre ways Christians have tried to affect their neighborhoods. One pastor pledged to spend three days locked in a six-foot plexiglass cube atop his church if more than four thousand people came to his Easter services. Another pastor, inspired by Evel Knievel, jumps buses in church parking lots on his motorbike, sometimes through a wall of fire. Yet another ran a Father's Day promotion in which fathers attending his church were offered raffle tickets with a chance to win one of two AR-15 rifles (fathers were also offered an extra ticket for every child they brought with them). Then, of course, there's the plethora of pastors who walk the roads carrying a huge wooden cross. And who could forget Ed Young's "Seven Days of Sex" stunt, where he urged couples in his twenty-thousand-member Fellowship Church in Grapevine, Texas, to follow him and his wife in a week of "congregational copulation," as he called it. In a follow-up gimmick in 2012, Young and his wife, Lisa, set up a bed on the church roof and pledged to spend twenty-four hours there together in front of God and everybody.[8]

Bemoaning these kinds of bizarre schemes, Chicago pastor Seth Tower Hurd recalls his own experience growing up as a young person in a stunt-crazy church.

> The "Christian Power Team" came to town and tore phone books in half, flexed their comically massive biceps, then threw in an altar call to commit to Jesus. Every Easter, my

family attended a "Passion Play," depicting the last hours of Jesus' life on the lawn of the courthouse, within viewing distance of three of the county's rowdiest bars. When I was a teen, one church brought in a female abstinence rapper (can't make that one up) to spit some sick verses about her lack of a sex life. This "hip-hop outreach" closed out with each high school student receiving a "sex can wait" cloth bracelet. (As you might imagine, many teens quickly found a variety of ways to modify these bracelets into ironic accessories saying things like "sex can't wait" or "sex can wait, masturbate.")[9]

Sometimes it feels like these stunts are a dime a dozen. But, as Hurd concludes, "church publicity stunts can just as easily make followers of Jesus look foolish, and arguably push nonbelievers even further from Christianity."[10] We agree, but on the other hand, you need to be cautious that in resisting the bizarre you don't opt for the boring.

For most of us, the bizarre examples we share above are not our usual experience of church. What's the alternative way of being the church in a world starving for an authentic expression of love in community? As we mentioned earlier, being a good neighbor is a great start, but it won't change the world. If we are serious about altering the world in which God has placed us, we need to find ways to deviate slightly from the script. It means we ask questions about motivation, hopeful outcomes, deeper purpose. We plant gardens, not just because we think they are pretty or we enjoy gardening as a hobby. Those reasons are not wrong, they just might be incomplete.

Tending to God's earth, for example, is much more holistic and may have a much greater impact in our context than we even imagine. In Vancouver, British Columbia, several members of Grandview Calvary Baptist Church tore up a parking lot on their church property to start a community garden, offering plot shares to neighbors and inviting various marginalized social groups to garden with them. The garden became a gathering place for unlikely neighbors to interact. It also became a therapeutic and life-giving activity for those who took up gardening as a part of healing and recovery from various forms of trauma, wounding or addiction. Tending to creation in this way was an outward expression of the church's value for sustainable food sourcing on a much wider scale. We cannot underestimate how these activities can shape the culture of our churches and contribute to shaping the culture of our neighborhoods.

If your neighbors see you and your spouse setting up a bed on the roof of your house to perform a week-long "sexperiment," chances are they won't be attracted to your faith. But if they only see you waving at them from the driveway, planting herb gardens in your front lawn or joining the Neighborhood Watch committee, we don't imagine they will be challenged to embrace any change either. As Thomas Moore says in his book *Soul Mates*, "It's my conviction that slight shifts in imagination have more impact on living than major efforts at change . . . deep changes in life follow movements in imagination."[11]

The kind of midwifing we're commending is the kind that goes beyond volunteerism and benign neighborliness. It attends to the deep longings of our neighbors and responds accordingly. Anthony and Toni Smith serve with Mission House, a missional community that styles itself as an "army of love" committed to the citywide renaissance of Salisbury, North Carolina. Anthony is also well known as the "postmodern negro," after his blog of the same name. They describe the DNA of the Mission House as incarnation, mission and reconciliation. By incarnation, they mean they are sent into their community as Christ was sent into the world. By mission, they mean they are sent by the Holy Spirit to join in God's renewal of our neighborhoods and cities. And by reconciliation, they mean they seek to be agents of peace in the midst of a long history of division and disunity. In other words, they are deeply resolved to enter deeply into the rhythms of life in and around Salisbury, not only to pour oil on the wounds of the broken, but also to be a divine disruption to the status quo.

For the past couple of years they've participated in a community-based prayer and presence group called Nightcrawlers. They meet every Friday night (weather permitting) to walk their community's streets and to talk with their neighbors, both young and old. They pray, sing, observe and listen to their community.

More recently, Anthony and the other Nightcrawlers have begun to survey their neighbors about the needs of the city. As they've done so, it has become apparent that the community is worn thin by street violence and by a sense of resignation that nothing can be done to change it.

After a person was shot and killed behind the American Legion Post in the West End, Anthony talked to his three-year-old grand-daughter who lives nearby. She had heard the gunshots. Anthony reports that she told him, "Grappy, they go pow pow."

Galvanized into action, Anthony and other local leaders are now developing a coordinated effort across the city to strengthen and reinvigorate neighborhood watch groups and other community groups. In doing so, they are embracing the work of collaborating with city government, churches and the leaders of neighborhood watch groups to gather and share best practices in maintaining a tight neighborhood of trust and looking out for each other.

In other words, the Smiths and Mission House are brokering a discussion about a sustained practice of deeply connected neigh-boring, one that gives more power to specific neighborhoods all across the city to become more safe and neighborly.

Anthony says, "An image has emerged of a quilt that has unravelled in the center and on the edges. Imagine if we had a neighborhood movement that sought to reweave the fabric of our neighborhoods. We can weave this fabric together!"

Recently, Anthony posted twelve lessons he's learned about faith-rooted community engagement. They read like a manual for mid-wives, helping to birth the new creation on the streets of our towns and neighborhoods across the country. They are a series of signposts for those hardy Christian souls committed to becoming a divine disruption to the dominant story of our broken world:

- Seek the face of God.
- Actively listen to the community.
- Discern the need(s).
- Join in mission with others.
- Expect opposition.
- Stay on mission.
- Stay inordinately prayerful.
- Ask powerful questions.
- Practice compassion with all community stakeholders.
- Be a student/servant in the margins of the community.
- Constantly cycle through the gospels.
- Be wise as serpents and harmless as doves.

As Anthony concludes, "All of this is love."[12]

4 MIDWIVES TO THE BIRTH OF THE NEW CREATION

Keep calm and call the midwife.

T-SHIRT SLOGAN

What God has birthed and is birthing are seeds of the new creation that will lead history to its true end. And the church has been invited to participate in the myriad ways God is changing our world. As provocative as it might be for the prophet Isaiah to refer to God as a woman in labor, we would like to introduce a fresh take on a metaphor to describe God's people—*midwives.* We think it's a metaphor that sheds new light on the endless, cunning negotiations the followers of Christ need to make with the culture in which they live.

It seems to us that much of the language we hear from Christians about changing the world stems from very masculine and militaristic imagery. No doubt, you've heard a well-meaning (male) church leader rallying his church by declaring that we are "at war" with society, or some iteration of that sentiment. I (Christiana) was once exhorted by another church leader, "You've got your band of brothers and you have to know your plan of attack, give your commands and lead your people forward." Militaristic imagery does find its way into Scripture and has served the church in reaching out in society (the Salvation Army, anyone?), but we believe these kinds of metaphors can only go so far. They would not have served the exiles in Babylon. Raising an army to combat Nebuchadnezzar's regime would have been foolhardy. Likewise, Jesus resisted the militaristic strategy of Barabbas and the zealots to overthrow the Roman Empire. Indeed, the early church did effectively "overthrow" Rome, not with military might but by following the impulses of the Spirit and reshaping culture slowly but surely from within.

Different metaphors have served the church more effectively than others at different times in church history. As Joseph Campbell was noted to have said, "If you want to change the world, you have to change the metaphor." But you need to choose the right metaphor. Mismatched metaphors can have dangerous implications. They can lead us astray as much as they can empower us. We want to suggest that today in America is no time for the church to be embracing militaristic campaigns of conquest. We're not proposing a ban on militaristic language, but we'd like to suggest the midwife as an additional metaphor that will deepen and expand the mystery of our faith and the reality of our calling. In fact, we think this metaphor can powerfully ignite our imagination for what God is birthing right before our eyes. God is giving birth to the new creation, and we have been invited to assist.

So what exactly is a midwife? A midwife is someone, most often a woman, trained to assist mothers in the process of labor, delivery and postpartum care. A certified nurse-midwife is a registered nurse with a master's degree in midwifery. In the United States, more than 90 percent of midwives practice in hospitals, while some work in birth centers or attend in home births. In most of the developed world, midwives are responsible for attending the majority of low-risk pregnancies.

Soon after the birth of my (Christiana's) second daughter, I would introduce my friend and midwife Janna as "my midwife who delivered my baby." Janna would respond, "I didn't deliver anything. It was *your* delivery of *your* baby, and I was privileged to assist in the birth." This reminds us precisely of the reason why we prefer the metaphor of midwifing over that of military combat. While a battle might be ours to win or lose, the role of the midwife is *always* dependent on the work of the delivering mother. Midwives don't actually give birth to anything. They simply assist. We believe God is birthing redemptive realities in our world, and we are summoned to assist in the miracle of new life.

The metaphor of the relationship between the midwife and the birthing mother depicts the Spirit of God as the one who carries life, delivers life and sustains life. As we've shown, Scripture describes God panting as a mother who gives birth to all things and nurtures life. In Numbers 11:12, as the Israelites complain of having only manna to eat in the wilderness, Moses says to God almost sarcastically, "Did I give birth to them? Did I bring them into the world? Why did you tell me to carry them in my arms like a mother carries a nursing baby? How can I carry them to the land you swore to give their ancestors?" (NLT). Moses' tone communicates that he perceives God as the one who gave birth to the Israelites and is therefore responsible to nurture them out of Egyptian bondage and in their wilderness experience.

Again in Isaiah 66:9 we see God portrayed as the one who gives birth, specifically to the newborn nation of Israel. "Would I ever bring this nation to the point of birth and then not deliver it?" (NLT). And in Isaiah 49:15, the prophet speaks the message of God: "Can a mother forget her nursing child? Can she feel no love for the child she has borne? But even if that were possible, I would not forget you!" (NLT). Once again, God is metaphorically correlated to one who gives birth and sustains life.

Jesus compares himself with a mother hen who cares for her chicks. "O Jerusalem, Jerusalem, the city that kills the prophets and stones God's messengers! How often I have wanted to gather your children together as a hen protects her chicks beneath her wings, but you wouldn't let me" (Lk 13:34 NLT). And in dialogue with Nicodemus Jesus refers to the Spirit as the one who gives birth. He says, "I assure you, no one can enter the Kingdom of God without being born of water and the Spirit. Humans can reproduce only human life, but the Holy Spirit gives birth to spiritual life" (Jn 3:5-6 NLT).

God the Spirit, who encompasses both feminine and masculine qualities and characteristics without being either a man or a woman, is birthing restorative structures, transformative communities and world-altering moments of love all around us. As we step into the redemption story of God, the way of the Christ lived in life today, we join the story, not as bystanders or even as recipients but as companions, giving out of what we've been given. Just as the midwife comes alongside a laboring mother, so we are invited to come alongside God in the miracle of birthing new life for the world around us. The task is not to get God to do something we think needs to be done, but to become aware of what God is doing so that we can participate in it.

THE ROLE OF THE MIDWIFE

The function of the midwife is an ancient one. Birthing mothers have been attended to by midwives for as long as we know. The ancient Jews called her the wise woman. The English term *midwife* is derived from Middle English *mit wif*, or "with-woman." In fact, the term *obstetrician* means to "stand in front of." It signifies one

who provides leadership, while the midwife (*with* woman) signifies partnership. Sheila Kitzinger describes her role as a midwife
this way:

> In all cultures the midwife's place is on the threshold of life,
> where intense emotions—fear, hope, longing, triumph and
> incredible physical power—enable a new human being to
> emerge. Her vocation is unique.
>
> The art of the midwife is in understanding the relation be-
> tween psychological and physiological processes in child-
> birth. . . . Her skills lie at the point where the emotional and
> biological touch each other and interact. She is not a manager
> of labour and delivery. Rather, she is the opener of doors, the
> one who releases, the nurturer. She is the strong anchor when
> there is fear and pain; the skilled friend who is in tune with
> the rhythms of birth, the mountain tops and chasms, the
> striving and the triumph.[1]

These attributes of a midwife apply not only in the birthing of a
child but also in the birthing, starting, pioneering, initiating and
creating of the things we dream about for this world. Many of us
look back on the things we've pioneered in our own vocational path,
and we can name the "midwives" who have come alongside us—
those heroes who have calmed our fears, awakened our hopes,
coaxed our longings, celebrated our triumphs and guided us
through our deepest pain and grief. Most of us know the blessing
of the accompanying stability that a metaphorical midwife provides
as we see new things birthed in the world.

Midwives are mentioned in Genesis 35, assisting Rachel as she
dies delivering her son Benjamin. And equally tragically, midwives
are mentioned in the beginning of Exodus when the Egyptian
Pharaoh demanded they murder all the newborn Hebrew sons:
"When you are helping the Hebrew women during childbirth on

the delivery stool, if you see that the baby is a boy, kill him; but if it is a girl, let her live" (Ex 1:16 NIV). The Hebrew midwives, Shiphrah and Puah, cannot bring themselves to undertake such a heinous task, so they allow the boys to live and cover their tracks by lying to Pharaoh: "Hebrew women are not like Egyptian women; they are vigorous and give birth before the midwives arrive" (Ex 1:19 NIV). The enslaved Hebrew community continued to thrive in Egypt in no small measure due to the caring midwifery of these heroic women.

However, by the Middle Ages, the midwife was viewed with great suspicion and fear. It was a superstitious time all around, of course, but for a woman to possess certain skills and abilities shrouded in mystery from the world of men who had nothing to do with childbirth, it became easy to explain their skills as coming from some spiritual force—indeed, some malevolent force. Some claimed the source of a midwife's ability must have come through an alliance with the devil. This led to many midwives being burned as witches.

Today, professional midwives are responsible for attending women during pregnancy, and in labor and birth. In fact, a 2013 medical review found that in the countries with the best pregnancy outcomes, midwives are the primary providers of care to pregnant women. Midwife-led care was associated with fewer interventions during birth and a decreased risk of losing the baby before twenty-four weeks' gestation or delivering prematurely. It concluded that "most women should be offered midwife-led continuity models of care and women should be encouraged to ask for this option."[2]

By preferring the metaphor of the midwife who attends as God births the new creation, we are not attempting to persuade anyone to choose a specific birth plan for their child, nor is this metaphor meant to ostracize anyone who has never physically given birth. As we stated earlier, the role of the midwife interacts beautifully with all forms of birthing and starting something meaningful in the world. Additionally, we don't mean to suggest God's work is as fragile as a newborn child, nor as dependent on us as a birthing mother is on her midwife. God's purposes can't be confounded. Nonetheless God's followers are graciously invited to join in the process of delivering new, redemptive realities in our world. That God is doing the birthing needs no defending. Psalm 139:13-15 implies that God is very present, even in utero: "You created my inmost being; you knit me together in my mother's womb. . . . My frame was not hidden from you . . . when I was woven together" (NIV).This thought is echoed by the prophet Jeremiah: "Before I formed you in the womb I knew you, before you were born I set you apart" (Jer 1:5 NIV). And the psalmist describes God delivering us: "You brought me out of the womb; you made me trust in you, even at my mother's breast" (Ps 22:9 NIV).

So, how is the metaphor of the midwife helpful in understanding our role as a culture-altering people? We think a number of implications can be taken from this metaphor, particularly by looking at the practices of midwifery and applying them to the church community today. In light of our concerns with rootless churches and colonizing methodologies of church planting, we'd like to offer some practices drawn from midwifery to provide an alternative vision for joining God in birthing the new creation.

MIDWIFE PRACTICE #1: RELEASING OUR AGENDAS

Foisting our agendas onto other people never works. Trying to change people or places without taking the time to genuinely listen beneath the surface is just never a good idea. Nearsighted agendas, even with the best of intentions, are a recipe for hurt and confusion at best.

A midwife is acutely aware of the fact that her own agendas, biases and ideals can and will impact the way in which she enters a birthing experience. Telling a birthing mother that she *must* do this, or feel that, or act in this particular way, will often be met by confusion or anger, disempowering the woman in her own birthing experiencing. There is a powerful force working in the laboring mother's body. Should the midwife seek to control the force, she runs the very real risk of stifling the actual thing she is called to foster. Midwives foster the birth of new life by intentionally releasing their agendas and respecting the force of birth.

A midwife is an integral part of a birth story. She enters the experience with an important role to play while recognizing her own boundaries and limits. She knows what her role is and what it is not. She must always listen to the laboring mother, to the environment, to others present and to the larger circumstances surrounding the place and time. These essential elements become guideposts that lead the midwife forward as she supports the birthing patterns.

A common tragedy we've seen in the Christian movement over the last couple decades is a programmatic approach to loving people or growing the church without entering into a context with a posture of listening. Midwives are good listeners. They don't make judgments by what they see on the surface or the observable tip of the iceberg, but they listen deeply for what is underneath the glistening surface of the water. The church was not sent to its neighborhood to control the situation. Rather, in the confidence that God is on the move in that neighborhood, the church midwifes the birth of the new creation. This requires a more attentive, less domineering stance.

Every community of faith desires to have a positive impact on its neighborhood. Most churches want to be an attractive, wooing presence that draws people to join their community and their cause. We are all familiar with church strategies such as erecting church signs, inviting people to church-sponsored events, enacting clean-up days or donating backpacks to the local schools. These are all great ideas and gestures. Yet surely the invitation of God is much more provocative and revolutionary than this. And it begins with attentive listening and releasing of our own agendas.

If we're honest, most of us don't always know exactly what it looks like to follow Jesus in the places where we live, work and recreate until we start doing it. We can't proceed with prefabricated programs and fixed assumptions about the shape of our churches. We must suspend our agendas and trust God more. Jesus himself was concerned that the message of God's good news be declared not simply with words but also by the performance of everyday acts of God's character, reliant on the power of the Spirit. The love of God is expressed by the very ordinary, everyday embodiment of real people in real places. Their exact shape can't be predetermined until we join God in those places, enacting God's agendas, not ours. We are called to be culture shapers, not simply give campaign speeches about love and peace or host events and send out mailers with a distant proclamation of the nature of God. We must also authentically embody the good news of love and peace in the nitty-gritty of life. This is the incarnation of the spirit of Christ. This is the agenda of God to which we attend.

MIDWIFE PRACTICE #2: SHAPING THE ENVIRONMENT

The nemesis to culture-shaping is culture-controlling. No one wants to claim to be a controlling person, yet we all, in one way or another, are constantly attempting to control something or someone with whatever power we think we have. We're control freaks, really. We try to control our appearance, our reputation, our food choices, our entertainment preferences, our friendships, our schedules, our money, our kids . . . the list goes on.

Try as we may, we'll never succeed in shaping the environments around us by trying to control them. As we release our agendas we begin to admit what we don't know, and we approach culture to listen and learn rather than to regulate. This is the beginning of shaping the environment to be conducive for birth. Midwives do this with excellence. They listen deeply as they create safe environments that prepare the way for the birth of new life.

Jesus of course modeled this midwife characteristic in the ways he shaped the environments he entered. Among many other stories, the way Jesus approached the Samaritan woman at the well in John 4 gives insight into his environment-shaping practice. He was present to the existing environment, walking through Samaria, a place other Jews would avoid because of unjust caste and ethnocentric bias. He was tired, hungry and thirsty, so he sat by the well, knowing that to fetch water he would need help from someone, most likely a woman. In a time when women were considered second-class to men, Jesus put himself in a vulnerable position by talking to her alone and depending on her for his needs. He spoke to the woman, not giving her demands or demeaning her like many others would have done, but by connecting with her heart, cutting through her cultural stature and her broken story, offering her a pattern of the abundant life that God intended for her. He believed in her and catalyzed real change through his presence, intentional actions and words.

Environment-shaping requires great intention. Intentionality means being faithfully present to everything around us. It means being led by the Spirit and, like a midwife in a delivery room, living an intentional life means we alert our eyes to keener sight, we listen attentively to every murmur and groan, and we look beyond surface behavior to see what a casual observer might miss completely.

When we approach the culture of a neighborhood, we have the opportunity to look intently for what the Spirit is doing and listen actively as we submerge below the surface in order to better understand the worldview out of which this culture finds its core rhythm. With this kind of intentionality we learn to live, moment to moment, out of our worldview of the kingdom of God, just as Jesus did.

But how do we follow in the way of Jesus and shape the environments we enter with the values of the kingdom of God? When churches commission foreign missionaries, they know that their first few years will be about adopting the language, understanding the culture's mores and folkways, learning how to behave in polite society and how to interpret cultural cues and signals. We expect crosscultural missionaries to learn the culture and be willing to patiently build authentic relationships if they're going to be trusted in the host country. If this is true for crosscultural mission, why do we so easily forget this important ingredient to incarnational mission in our own home contexts?

As we intentionally immerse our lives in the cultures around us we will face choices that present opportunities to pause and listen before we act. Without pause, we enter into dangerous territory where our ideals can consume and destroy even the tiniest seeds of goodness that are growing within that environment. Allow us to share two stories to illustrate some contrasting approaches for how the followers of Jesus may seek to shape our environments with the good news of God's love. These stories illustrate our first two midwifing practices, with more to come in the following chapters.

In San Diego, a lead pastor and his wife decided to jump through the hoops necessary to be elected to the community development corporation (CDC) of the neighborhood where their church building sits. Local civic involvement is one of their church's goals to impact their city with the gospel. The majority of the church members, including the pastor and his family, live in other neighborhoods a good distance from where they attend church each week. Aside from their church facilities and the events they occasionally host in their parking lot or fellowship hall throughout the year, the people who make up this church have minimal natural overlap or investment in the well-being of the local context where they meet throughout the week. In the previous chapter, we referred to this as a rootless church. Although they are stakeholders in the general economy of the neighborhood by virtue of owning property and meeting there regularly, they haven't yet made the kind of personal, relational investment that comes from having a shared sense of geographical identity with their neighbors.

With this background in mind, we can report that the pastor and his wife sat on the CDC for many months, speaking up on decisions, sharing opinions, taking on needed tasks and roles and offering their church building for community events and meetings. They were earnest in giving of their time and resources. They believed that hosting neighborhood meetings and events at their church would be a prime opportunity to display the love of God. In their minds, it would save the CDC money as the facilities could be offered free of charge. And church members could cook food and volunteer their time as a service to the wider community. As generous as this offer was, though, the pastor and his wife were met with opposition from the rest of the CDC, who felt that hosting any neighborhood event in a church building would communicate a religious affiliation that could ostracize segments of the community and diminish their attempts to create an inclusive invitation for neighborhood community building.

The pastoral couple couldn't understand this resistance to their kind offer. They remained diplomatic but they refused to back down, insisting that the church facilities would be a perfect asset. Soon, polite disagreement became a rumbling of confusion and ultimately disunity around the table. It all came to a head when enough people stepped down from the CDC because of the tension, leaving major responsibilities in the hands of the clergy couple, who saw it as an opportunity to finally impact the neighborhood with the good news of Jesus like they never had before. Freed from opposition and a responsibility to run truly inclusive events, the couple took on the task of heading up the annual neighborhood festival. What resulted was astounding.

The CDC received a substantial grant to spend on the festival, which the church couple appropriately allocated, giving a large percentage to the entertainment portion of the event. In years past, the entertainment at this event was filled with local bands, artists and musicians from all over San Diego that represented varied ethnic backgrounds, spiritual perspectives and music genres. This year, however, the stage took on a completely different flavor, not at all reflecting the culture of the neighborhood or the immediate surrounding urban area. Every act—musicians, solo singers, mimes, speeches, dance—explicitly gave glory to Jesus Christ their Lord and Savior. But none of it was birthed out of the neighborhood itself.

The church couple considered this a great evangelistic success. The rest of the neighborhood, however, was left disoriented and disappointed. From our point of view, we would say that the predetermined agendas that this church couple brought to the CDC, and the impact their actions had on the neighborhood and its people, actually hindered the very life that God was birthing in that place. While the church couple had the best of intentions (local civic involvement and evangelism are worthwhile causes), they were largely ignorant of how to read the position they found themselves in. Their ultimate refusal to listen, or to adopt the posture of the midwife by suspending judgment and releasing their agendas, meant that the spark of life they might have helped fan into flame flickered out. Genuine opportunities for meaningful and potentially impactful sharing of the message of Jesus could have been facilitated far more effectively if the couple had taken a slower, more relational, more collaborative approach to joining the CDC.

During and after the festival, the online neighborhood discussion board blew up with complaints, confusion and even outrage over what the CDC endorsed as a neighborhood event. One such comment read, "I don't understand. This was an imposter, pretending to be one of us but reflecting nothing of our true identity as a neighborhood." At the next CDC meeting, the community confronted the couple, telling them in no uncertain terms that the festival had been a false representation of who they are. Of course, in similar circumstances, Christians often interpret such opposition as religious persecution, that "the world" is attacking us because we are disciples of Jesus. Didn't Jesus even promise this would happen? But the kind of culture-altering posture we are calling the church to is about genuine listening that allows us, if indeed we are going to offend our neighbors, to do so for the proper biblical reasons, not for being bad neighbors or for being pushy members of our local community development committees. Jesus said we will be persecuted for righteousness' sake, not for obnoxiousness' sake.

This may seem like an extreme scenario, but unfortunately, stories like this are all too common. The church has a habit of stumbling into settings they don't know with a medium for their message that only alienates and repels. It looks nothing like Jesus. Truthfully, we've all done it to one degree or another. We believe it is time to repent of our addiction to cultural control and humble ourselves as servants, embracing the way of the cross of Christ that summons us to release our very lives for love. In other words, it is time to adopt the posture of the midwife.

The second story we want to share illustrates the alternative posture to that of the "invade and control" model that seems to dominate much of our evangelistic imagination. Eric and Lisa Purcell and their two young children intentionally moved into the neighborhood of Gifford Park, Omaha, Nebraska, with a desire to love God in the neighborhood, to form an intentional community centered on Christ and invest their lives in their place by joining God's activity of restoration and renewal.

Eric and Lisa founded a community ministry, working to form leaders who create and nurture Christ-centered communities embedded in neighborhoods around the world. During their first couple of years in Gifford Park, the Purcells volunteered and participated in events, initiatives and services that were already happening in the neighborhood. They joined in community garden work days, community clean-up days, neighborhood-wide garage sales, summer tennis programs, ESL programs helping refugee neighbors and many more initiatives that were already at play in Gifford Park. As relationships were forged, Eric was invited onto the Neighborhood Association Board, and after serving for one year he was elected president. Eric describes the experience as an overwhelming honor, acknowledging that the role entrusted to him came with great responsibility to steward the neighborhood for the common good.

Eric's position as the board president gave him great influence on decisions, overseeing projects that had a direct impact in the flourishing of their place, their friends and their family. From forging cultural celebrations with the local ESL program to establishing the neighborhood as a 501(c)(3) for more philanthropic endeavors, Eric and the neighborhood leadership pioneered important changes to better their shared context.

What is especially encouraging to us is how Eric and Lisa's faith has governed their actions as contributing neighbors in Gifford Park. In order to discover God's purposes for their place, they embraced a variety of contemplative actions, including listening for God's guidance in silence and meditation, walking their streets in prayer as they looked for God's transformation in their place at the deepest levels, and offering a listening ear for those in need of a friend. In one particular instance, while on a prayer walk, Eric and Lisa began to dream about what it might look like to work with the city to creatively turn an abandoned lot into usable land for the neighborhood. They prayed for two years as this piece of land filled with piles of concrete and mounds of dirt sat as an eyesore and underutilized resource. After much work together with the Neighborhood Association they finally got approval from the city to transform this land into a public permanent soccer field for the neighborhood residents.

The Purcells and their growing community of Jesus followers have become spiritual friends to numerous people over the years, caring for felt needs and tending to souls. After they purchased their home, a neighbor knocked on their door holding up the key to his own home and said, "Now that you own your home we know you really care about this place; we know we can trust you." The Purcells are walking beside this neighbor as he's aligning his life with Jesus.

Eric and Lisa had to take intentional steps to engage their surrounding culture. They embraced the midwifing practices of choosing to release their agendas and choosing to pause and listen as the first and ongoing step to shaping their environment. This doesn't usually come naturally. In fact, if we're not intentional, we run the risk of hindering the birthing process without even realizing we're doing it!

These two stories illustrate the difference between the problems that the church faces today (Sunday-centric, rootless, controlling approaches to mission) and the steps needed to overcome those problems (abandoning control, releasing agendas, shaping the environment). As we mentioned in the first two midwifing practices, releasing our agendas requires a meticulous process of acknowledging our preconceived notions, opinions, prejudices and the lenses through which we interpret the world around us. Learning to shape our environments, making them conducive for birth, requires a circumspect attentiveness to the existing culture and careful infusing of the values of God. In the next couple of chapters we will explore more midwifing practices for attending God in the birth of the new creation.

5 MAKING SPACE FOR BIRTH TO HAPPEN

*Mission is, quite simply, the participation of
Christians in the liberating mission of Jesus,
wagering on a future that verifiable experience
seems to belie. It is the good news of God's love,
incarnated in the witness of a community,
for the sake of the world.*

DAVID BOSCH

The classical Greek philosopher Socrates (470–399 BC) was
noted for asking questions. Today, his style of teaching is referred
to as the Socratic method—the posing of a series of questions to help
students figure out their underlying beliefs and to eventually eliminate faulty hypotheses and find better ones. Socrates himself regularly used two metaphors to describe his contribution to Athenian
society. One was that of the "gadfly, the horsefly that stings the intel-
lectually and morally sluggish citizens of Athens with his questioning.
'For Athens is a great and noble steed that is tardy in its motions.'"[1]

The other metaphor he used to describe his work is that of the midwife who helps others give birth to the wisdom that he believed was within everyone. He explained it this way in *The Theaetetus* (150 BC): "My art of midwifery is in general like theirs [real midwives]; the only difference is that my patients are men, not women, and my concern is not with the body but with the soul that is in travail of birth. And the highest point of my art is the power to prove by every test whether the offspring of a young man's thought is a false phantom or instinct with life and truth."[2]

He assumed the ability to find the truth was within all people (well, men in his culture), and that his questions prompted this truth to become fully gestated and ultimately birthed into society. Interestingly, he was of the view that "the heavens" had prohibited him from teaching wisdom directly, from presenting fully formed philosophical truths to his students. Rather, his job was to stand alongside those students, creating the space into which they could give birth to wisdom:

> Those who frequent my company at first appear, some of them, quite unintelligent, but, as we go further with our discussions, all who are favored by heaven make progress at a rate that seems surprising to others as well as to themselves, although it is clear that they have never learned anything from me. The many admirable truths they bring to birth have been discovered by themselves from within. But the delivery is heaven's work and mine.[3]

For those male readers who are anxious that the metaphor of a midwife might not apply to them, think of the culture-shaping work of Socrates. It is a beautiful symbol of the work the church must do—to cooperate with God who is birthing the new creation. We do not give birth to anything ourselves. That is God's work. But as attendants to the birth, there are several other important functions that the church needs to embrace. In the previous chapter we looked at how the church needs to suspend its prefabricated models of ministry and respond to the impulses of the Spirit in the particular place in which it is planted. But more than that, we think the church needs to do as Socrates did and create space for birth. Socrates did it with questions. The church will do it a little differently.

MIDWIFE PRACTICE #3: HOLDING THE SPACE FOR BIRTH

In the last hour of labor before my (Christiana's) second child was born I experienced firsthand the settling presence of a skilled midwife. There was a profound sense of welcome as I climbed the stairs of the birth center and rounded the corner to see my midwife, Janna, walking confidently toward me with open arms. She gave me a warm and reassuring hug, gently guiding me toward where I could best continue my labor process. "Your baby is coming," Janna whispered. It was in the middle of the night, and I was dog-tired and uncomfortable. She dimmed the lights and set the room temperature just warm enough to create a calming and inviting space for relaxation and focus. There was a tranquility that caught me off guard. My midwife held the space for birth, and forty-five minutes after I arrived, on February 23, 2010, Anika Mae was born into the world.

There's a mantra used by midwives that goes, "We are to hold the space for birth." Nurturing an environment conducive to birth is a key role of the midwife. She looks at a space to determine its assets and its liabilities. She creates an inviting setting of welcome and nurture, protecting the space, removing potential barriers as best she can, whether they be physical, systemic, spiritual or relational. A midwife shields a birthing mother from anything that may hinder the birthing process. Her presence alone shifts the energy of a room, making it possible for an optimum, healthy birth experience even in the most challenging of circumstances. She is a guardian of birth.

Just as a midwife holds the space for new life, so the church is called to hold the space in our neighborhoods, towns and cities for the Spirit to give birth to the new creation. Our contexts are both fertile for birth and vulnerable to that which steals life. We are called to nurture and protect the life that God is forming in our place. Just as a midwife arranges spaces conducive to birth, followers of Christ can learn to develop the practice of "reading" a place and assessing how favorable it may be to receiving the new life God is birthing.

Some years ago, I (Michael) spent some time with John Hayes, the founder of InnerCHANGE, a Christian order among the poor. John and Deanna were living in a poor neighborhood in San Francisco at the time, and I had gone to ask them to help me explore the contours of incarnational mission. John's writing emphasizes the importance of relocating to be among the poor, rather than visiting them to deliver aid from more affluent suburbs, which can send a message to the poor community that their environment is "too toxic for 'good' Christians to live in."[4] Yet relocating to be among the poor is challenging. It means making different choices about the educational options for your children, and it limits your own employment options considerably. Of course, it means negotiating your way through neighborhoods that can be less than safe. I anticipated spending a lot of time engaging with his neighbors and digging into the minutiae of his everyday life. Instead, he threw me in his car and drove me all over San Francisco.

He took me to China Beach, nestled under the hillside mansions of the Sea Cliff neighborhood. Here, he explained, the Chinese workers who had flooded to San Francisco to work during the gold rush were forced to live in substandard makeshift camps in what was referred to as the "Outside Lands," enforced by the Chinese Exclusion Act of 1902. The act is referred to as "to that point the country's most racist immigration law."[5]

From there John drove me over to Civic Center to view the controversial Pioneer Monument with its famously demeaning portrayal of native peoples, the triumvirate of Mexican vaquero, Franciscan padre and the submissively seated Indian. As we stood in the shadow of what has been called the most politically incorrect statue in the United States, John explained the historical cycles of oppression, from Native Americans, through the Mexicans and the missionaries, to the development of modern San Francisco.

Then we visited the Mission District and the Tenderloin, while John pointed out the charitable work of the Franciscan missions and current Catholic Worker communities. He showed how Market Street bisected the city from Civic Center, the seat of power, straight down to the ferry terminal, the lifeblood of the city. Then he drove me up to Twin Peaks so I could imagine the old patterns etched into the city landscape—the Chinese huddled far off to the west in the Outside Lands, the poor crammed into the areas south of Market, and the wealthy to the north in Nob Hill and Russian Hill.

Frankly, it was all too much to take in. He spent a long time unfolding the historical and geographic landscape of his city. Initially, I found this frustrating. What was he doing giving me this history lesson like I was some tourist? But later, when we hung out in his neighborhood, things started to become clear. He saw himself as curating a place, a space in which God would work among the poor. Knowing the city's history of oppression and marginalization and understanding its effect on the built environment allowed John to know how best to "hold the space" for what God wanted to do.

STUDYING YOUR PLACE

Informed by the work of Michael Mata, professor of transformational urban leadership at Azusa Pacific University in Los Angeles, InnerCHANGE members have utilized what he calls the five S's to studying your place. They are Structures, Signs, Spatial dynamics,

Social interaction and Spirituality. And InnerCHANGE takes all five very seriously. How can you, like a midwife, hold the space for God to birth new redemptive possibilities without considering these things? Expanding on what we've learned from Mata and InnerCHANGE, let us briefly lay out some components to each of these S's as we've understood them, providing questions you can ask in engaging the elemental dynamics in your place.

1. Structures. When learning the story of our place, we pay attention to what the structures or buildings are like. This is exactly what John Hayes was doing with me in San Francisco. He was showing me what the built environment was telling him about mission in that city. The built environment fosters certain environmental components that have the potential to build and enhance community or to destroy it. Be conscious of the different districts or neighborhoods in your city. Districts are areas with perceived internal sameness—neighborhoods, public housing zones, etc. Also, look for the structural edges of a place, the dividing lines between districts. They are the linear elements not used or considered as paths by the observer, but which separate districts. They might be freeways, rivers, train lines—anything that determines the edge of a district. And be aware of important landmarks. As a regular visitor to San Francisco, I (Michael) have walked or driven past the Pioneer Monument several times without even noticing the implied message of racism and oppression in its symbolism. It took a local to point it out. Other landmarks might be points of reference such as well-known or loved buildings, signs, stores, mountains, rivers, etc.

When studying the structures of your neighborhood or city, ask the following questions:

- What are the actual structures that exist in this neighborhood, and what kinds of people are they built for?
- What is their purpose?

- When were they built, and what funding was used to build them?
- Are the structures older or new, well kept or run down, rented or owned, businesses, third spaces or services?
- Are there fences, bars or walls?

2. Signs. What is written or painted in a neighborhood tells a greater story than we are often conscious of. Intentionally taking the time to look will open our eyes to notice what we often overlook. Billboards, advertisements, graffiti, tagging, bumper stickers and political signs are all unique to each place. Reading beneath what is written helps us to better understand the demographics, diversity, voices and values of a place. Some signs provide needed resources, instruction or stated values for positive change. Others communicate violence, desperation, boredom, isolation or self-protection. Others still provide doorways into your neighborhood. Some years ago, I (Michael) visited a neighborhood where one of my students was ministering. As we drank coffee in a local café I saw a sign above a second-story building across the road that read, "The oldest continually run gym in all of Sydney!" It wasn't a downtown neighborhood. It was an outer suburb, an unlikely place for a historic gym to be situated. When I pointed the sign out to him, my former student blinked. He'd never noticed it before. Nonetheless, he followed my suggestion that we go and talk to the proprietor. It turns out that Tony, the elderly gym owner, had been running a gym in that suburb for over fifty years. He knew everyone who lived there and understood the history of the community like no one else. He eventually became a wonderful conduit for my former student, now a local pastor, to connect to his neighbors, and all simply because we actually read a sign.

We need to do what Thomas Troeger called "alerting the eye to keener sight"[6] by becoming aware of the messages we receive from the images with which we live, and by assessing how those images are shaping our political and social perspective. If we get this right, we'll be better able to develop appropriate responses to the challenges and opportunities they pose. When studying signs, consider asking these questions:

- Are there themes to the signs you see in the neighborhood?
- Who are they mostly catering to, and for what purpose?
- Did it cost money to make this statement or mark or advertisement?
- What are the dominant languages used, values communicated and affiliations represented through these signs in the neighborhood?

3. Spatial dynamics. The spatial layout of any environment can foster relational interaction or snuff it out. Consider airport gate lounges, with their fixed lines of seating all facing the same direction, the lack of tables or group spaces and the dominance of screens. Their spatial layout makes them inconducive to interaction. They're designed in a way that assumes you're not here to stay, you're just passing through. Likewise, in most neighborhoods some degree of planning has gone into creating the environment in which people live, work and play. Some places have more resources and infrastructure than others, of course. Some were built with a specific vision in mind, and others were pieced together after decades of hardship and economic shifts. Spaces matter because they have the ability to draw people together or reinforce independence. Space can celebrate nature or degrade it. Space can encourage social and economic diversity or push people away from each other.

In studying your space, you need to be aware of any well-worn paths that are used in your neighborhood. Paths are the channels along which people customarily, occasionally or potentially move (streets, walkways, public transport lines, rivers, railways, etc.). The paths we take shape and distort our perspective on the city. Look out for nodes as well—places where multiple paths intersect, such as primary junctions, marketplaces, plazas, bus stations, metro stops, intersections, etc. Ask these questions when studying space:

- Does the space communicate density, hospitality, privacy or self-protection?
- Are there wide open spaces and, if so, what do they say about the values of this particular neighborhood?
- Are there spaces for recreation or spaces that honor nature?
- Is it easily walkable or bike friendly?
- What does public transportation look like in this place, and is it a primary space taker or on the periphery of society?
- Are streets wide or narrow, and are there alleys, yards and empty lots?
- As a resident of the neighborhood, in what ways is your own sense of relational connectedness dependent on the spatial dynamics of your place?

4. Social interaction. It is imperative that followers of Christ, trying to hold the space for the birth of the new creation to happen, be aware of how social interactions occur in their neighborhood. Obviously, the built environment is key in fostering or hindering social interaction, as indeed is the natural environment. Some social interaction is instinctual, given certain dynamics and realities of an environment. Other interactions happen simply by cultural norms and expectations of what it means to be a neighbor in any given context. Studying social interaction tells us what degree of interdependence this place values and how these interactions affect everyday life together. It takes a while to pick up on this, though. It will require you to spend a lot of time hanging out in nodes, watching interactions, observing conversations between different kinds of people, and when, how and why they interact. Often these questions can be pondered by walking and observing the pace of your place, whether or not people recreate or hang out in visible spaces. Check to see whether windows and curtains are open or closed. Do people seem to welcome interruptions, or is privacy a high value? For some places, these questions will have different answers for different households or even different streets. Some folks may not have cars or may live outdoors or simply come through the neighborhood regularly to recycle from trash bins. There can be many different expressions and experiences held in one neighborhood. It's important not to overgeneralize any of our conclusions and commit to being ongoing learners in our place.

Recently, one of my (Michael's) students led her church through an intensive examination of the social interactions in her parish. Called the "Love Your Neighbour" project, members of the church walked the streets of their region to get a better understanding of: (a) the character of the different neighborhoods in their parish, (b) the movement of local people at different times of the day and days of the week and (c) potential connection points where people gather and find community. They mapped their parish, took photographs, interviewed community leaders and listened to locals.[7] These are questions to ask when undertaking such a study of social interactions:

- Are there pedestrians? If it's a walking culture, are they walking for leisure, walking pets or heading to somewhere like a neighbor's house or the park or the store or a community center? Or is walking a form of transportation out of the neighborhood? When walkers pass each other do they greet one another or pass with an ignoring silence?

- Do people just drive through to get to another destination?

- Are the people on the streets locals or visitors? If they're visiting, what usually brings them to the neighborhood?

- Where do people hang out?

- Are there outdoor spaces, indoor spaces, spaces that foster interaction and spaces that allow for independent activities?

- What kinds of people make up your neighborhood? Elderly, children, teenagers, young adults, middle-aged folks? Is there an obvious socioeconomic and ethnic diversity? Is there a diversity of self-expression, or do most people look similar?

- Is it a hostile or friendly environment? Are there signs of social conflict or neighborhood identity and unity? Do people seem to know their neighbors, and do they want to know them?

5. *Spirituality.* Spirituality is lived out in all sectors of society. It is sometimes difficult to parse what is spiritual and what is considered nonspiritual, but for the sake of this process we will use "spirituality" to refer to the ways in which humanity interacts with the unseen world, the inner life, God, spirit and their concept of life after death. Examining what people worship, how people worship, where they worship and how their worship affects their everyday life is imperative to better understanding our place and gaining insight into what influences our place as a "force" or "energy" or "spirit" for good or for evil. As we dig deeper in understanding what influences are at play in our place, we will uncover the unseen fury that affects the places we inhabit. Some may call this "bad or good energy," others may use the terms "territorial spirits" or "forces of good and evil." No matter how we express it, most of us can agree that there are unseen elements that take up residence in a place. So how do we become aware of those elements that influence the environment and therefore act to hold the space for more goodness, justice and redemption to be birthed?

Here are some questions for studying your local spirituality:

- What are the formal places of worship in the neighborhood? When and how were they built or started? Are they well attended?

Are those who attend a worship service from the neighborhood or do they commute in?

- What other spiritual groups gather in your neighborhood? Where do they gather?
- Are there spiritual gatherings in parks, coffee shops, homes or rented rooms? How do you know they're there?
- What kinds of spiritual postings do you see on community notice boards, at cafés or restaurants or on telephone poles? What kinds of services are provided in your neighborhood for spiritual seeking, meditation, service to the poor, activism or help groups?
- Do people proselytize or go door to door?
- Are there debates, discussions or conflicts over beliefs?
- What are places of solace in the neighborhood where people go for silence, solitude and meditation? Where can one go for prayer, spiritual readings, fortunetelling or religious classes?

Remember, you're undertaking this work like a midwife, assessing the environment and attentive to every aspect of the space. This is work churches expect missionaries to do in a new culture, but churches can shift their interest and begin doing this in their own contexts as well. By remaining ignorant of the space you inhabit, you are less able to see what God is doing, or determine what God wants to do in that environment.

But we would like to add a sixth S to Mata's list that, we believe, will make us even better students of our place. While it's not one of the five S's, it was very much part of what John Hayes was doing with me (Michael) that day in San Francisco. The sixth S is Story. In order to understand our present, we must sift through our past. For a neighborhood context, learning the long-range backstory gives insight into existing dynamics today.

6. Story. The macro story of a place has a lasting impact on its personality, general culture, strength and liability. Without knowing a story we fall prey to the possibility of misjudging a place for what it is not. The strength of a place can come from its resilient past, surviving great strife and hostility to get to where it is today. The liabilities of a place can come from a burdensome past where the oppressive realities around it have pushed it so far down that it perpetually walks with a limp. These kinds of stories behind everyday realities need to be excavated and retold. While interpreting signs, studying spirituality or examining structures can be tricky, learning the story of your city isn't that difficult at all. Visit city hall. See if they have a historian or an archivist. Talk to the public librarians. Meet long-term residents. Read history books. Search for online resources. Make it your business to know the actual history of your neighborhood. Ask the following questions:

- What are the stories being told by the long-term residents and business owners?

- What stories were told to them?

- What have they seen, and what do they predict about the future of that place?

- When studying historical documents or news reports from as far back as available, what significant stories stand out?

- How did this place get its name? You'd be surprised how many people don't know this.

- What patterns do you notice as you trace the lasting and changing values of a place?

- What cycles seem to dominate and obstruct the imagination of a place?

- What fuels aspiration, fear, drive and despair, and what are the prevailing stories of hope that linger there?

The study of place informs the way we pray for our neighbors, the way we extend love and the way we can contend for God's kingdom to come on earth as it is in heaven. We're not necessarily proposing that what is discovered in this process will lead directly to some sort of radical undertakings. But it's like falling in love—this learning process can lead us to accept what we still do not know and from there, choose love in the everyday simplicity of what we've discovered. And of course, there is always time to discover more on the path of faithfulness. We must never assume that we've reached a complete understanding of our place. The story of our place continues to be written. Its history continues to be uncovered. If we are not careful, we can fall into the trap of thinking we've figured out our neighborhood and we know exactly what it will take to save it. Let us be clear here: we can *never* know all there is to know about our place. Yet the more we discover, the more we can love with sincerity and wisdom.

John Hayes has dedicated the last thirty years of his life to living and serving among the poor and to forming leaders to incarnate the good news of Jesus in suffering contexts around the world. In his book *Sub-merge*, he describes an important aspect of incarnational ministry as a process of careful adjustments, where we are ever shifting to better understand our context, delve into deeper relationships and help meet the greater needs of our neighbors. He writes, "If we lose sight of incarnational ministry as a process of careful adjustments, then we threaten our sustainability, our joy in the adventure and our relationships with our neighbors."[8] So this kind of incarnational ministry is not just a straight line from us to those to whom we've been sent. It is a web of interconnecting relationships that offer the possibility of joy and the relational blessing we receive from those we are living among.

As we learn more about our place, we become conduits of goodness and grace, holding the space for God's Spirit to birth redemptive realities and build hope. We connect people in need with resources that could best serve them. We cultivate gathering spaces that nurture human connection. We tell people about Jesus. We treat people as Jesus would. We offer dignity and worth to all kinds of neighbors. We find ways to communicate the untold stories, we stand up against unjust systems that oppress the weak and marginalized, and we learn what it means to be good and faithful friends, heralding peace at every turn.

SMALL BOAT BIG SEA IN MANLY

As my (Michael's) community Small Boat Big Sea (SBBS) has engaged in mapping our neighborhood and learning its story, interesting connections have been made. SBBS is situated in Manly, on Sydney's north shore. The town got its name in an unusual way. The first British governor of Sydney, Arthur Phillip, rowed across the harbor in 1788, exploring the waterways of the new colony.[9] When he landed on the north shore he was met with some resistance by the indigenous people he found living in the area, so he recorded in his diary, "Their confidence and manly behaviour made me give the name of Manly Cove to this place." A year later, smallpox—brought to Australia by the British colonists—had all but wiped out the Guringai people that Governor Phillip had declared so manly. By the 1830s, only a few Guringai remained in the area. There's a bitter irony to living in a town named after the manly Guringai, whose constitutions were no match for the bugs brought by the colonists.

But the real history of the town of Manly starts much later, in 1853, when an enterprising young businessman named Henry Gilbert Smith arrived. Until then, the Manly area was inhabited by the dwindling Guringai and a very small population of colonists, eking out a sad living from fishing or farming the claylike ground of the area. Smith was a P. T. Barnum–like character, a raconteur and showman who thought that the sheltered beachside cove seven miles across the water from the smog and bustle of Sydney would be a perfect entertainment hub for the colony. He set about purchasing large tracts of land with a vision of Manly becoming "the favorite resort of the Colonists." He started a ferry service across the harbor, built hotels and donated land for schools and churches. He also built a camera obscura, a maze and a large stone kangaroo to attract visitors (tourists were more easily pleased in those days!). In June 1855, Smith wrote to his brother in England, "The amusement I derive in making my improvements in Manly is, no doubt, the cause of my greater enjoyment, in fact, I never feel a dull day while there. . . . I am thinking I am doing good in forming a village or watering place for the inhabitants of Sydney."

Manly became the Las Vegas of nineteenth-century Sydney. Smith oversaw the development of dance halls, amusement parlors, water slides and even a New Zealand Maori cultural performance (who can imagine what the manly Guringai people thought of all that!). He installed a large sign over the ferry terminal that greeted visitors upon arrival: "Manly—Seven Miles from Sydney, and a Thousand Miles from Care." It reminds me of the sign in the Las Vegas airport: "What Happens in Vegas, Stays in Vegas." The Guringai had been decimated by disease and their traditional tribal lands had been converted into an entertainment precinct for tourists and drunken Sydney residents.

In 2008, it was announced that Manly had the highest incidence of alcohol-fueled violence in the whole state. The local police chief said that Saturday nights in Manly were like a perpetual spring break. He described it as a "war zone." The story of Manly was coming home to roost. But more than its history, the town's structures contributed to the problem too. In the 1970s, the main street had been paved and converted into a pedestrian mall with pubs and bars lining either side of the street. Drunken teens and young adults spilled out of the pubs into a crowded paved space, almost purpose-built to lead to jostling and shoving. Furthermore, the only public transportation hub was located at the west end of the street, which meant these tired, drunk young people were funneled in the same direction toward the taxis, buses and ferry. The built environment seemed to be designed to foster violence.

The mayor of Manly declared it a disaster and established a campaign to curb late night violence in the main street. She increased policing, installed CCTV cameras and forced publicans to take courses in the responsible serving of alcohol. Nothing worked. She asked local high schools to offer classes in the dangers associated with excess drinking, to no effect. She even started hosting family-style activities and concerts in the main street on Saturdays to attract kids and families to try to dispel the culture of excess drinking, carousing and fighting. No one came. She spent over a million dollars trying to address the problem with no success. Was it any wonder? Any cursory study of the story of Manly would reveal that the roots of alcohol and excess went all the way back to the very establishment of the town itself. The sands of the beachside community were soaked with blood and booze. Changing it would require far more than a few CCTV cameras and extra police.

What catalyzed my (Michael's) involvement in this issue was hearing that one of the local ministers was intending to approach the mayor to get the funding to host "alcohol free, top quality Christian concerts" in the main street every Saturday night. The minister's rationale was that when our neighbors saw the Christian community having a fun and enjoyable night with great music and no booze, they would be attracted to our way of life. Aside from the obvious practical problems (they wanted to host the concerts at 8 p.m. when the real problems began well after midnight), this proposal clearly didn't take the story of Manly into account. They were going to combat violent, drunken partying with nonviolent, sober partying. They weren't going to seriously address the culture of carousing in any way. I felt I couldn't lend my weight to this suggestion, something that distressed a few of the ministers greatly.

Eventually, a small band of local church leaders managed to convince the promoters of the weekly Christian concert idea to let us try something different. We set about bringing the neighborhood together to rediscover their history and to dream of a new future for Manly. We invited the mayor, the police chief, the head of the chamber of commerce and the local pub owners to explore our options. It became a long and involved process, but synergies and collaborative processes slowly started to emerge. It's a long story, but suffice to say that none of them were interested in a top quality Christian concert. Instead we convinced some of the publicans to change their business model (the most violent pub had been holding midnight wet T-shirt contests), helping them to see that the violence was actually limiting their financial return, not enhancing it. We worked on developing different public transportation options, including the employment of bus and taxi "monitors" who helped quell aggression among patrons.

But the greatest and most effective initiative we started was the recruitment of hundreds of local people to act as "street pastors." Wearing blue uniforms clearly emblazoned with the words "street pastor," these hardy volunteers patrol the main street and the entertainment precinct in pairs or groups of four from midnight until 4 a.m. with a mandate to "listen, help and care" for the revelers of Manly. They don't break up fights. They don't make arrests. They don't ask people to move on. They sit in the gutter and listen to intoxicated teens crying because their boyfriend is dancing with another girl. They help inebriated revelers walk to the taxi hub. They clean up vomit and pick up broken glass. They just listen, help and care. And within a year, the rate of alcohol-related violence dropped by one third, and has continued to drop ever since.

God wanted to birth peace on the streets of Manly. God wanted to deliver love and grace and kindness to this dark place. All we did was curate the space. All we did, like any midwife, was rearrange the conditions to facilitate God's birthing work. We assessed the space. We learned the history. We listened carefully.

Knowing our place evokes our imagination for another future. The future that God intends has the power to redeem past pain and evoke enduring beauty. Every place and its story has a purpose and gift to offer the world. We are a part of the story that God is writing in our place. It doesn't begin and end with us. And as David Whyte says in his poetic brilliance, "We are the ending of some stories, the carrying on of others, and often just the beginning of many it is not our place to finish."[10]

6

ON BEING ADAPTIVE AND DARING

You never change things by fighting the existing reality. To change something, build a new model that makes the existing model obsolete.

BUCKMINSTER FULLER

Changing our world means cooperating with the redemptive possibilities God is birthing around us. As we noted, that involves abandoning our preconceived notions of what ministry should look like and entering fully into the contexts in which God has placed us. Our very presence will cause ripples. If we truly enter our contexts we will be a disruption to the status quo. The temptation when those unsettling repercussions occur is to retreat back into tried and true models of mission (running events, controlling the culture). Learning to release our agendas, become culture shapers and hold the space as we trust God with birthing the new creation is difficult. It takes focus, faith and intention. It requires nimble adaptability and daring courage, the very qualities we see in the Old Testament exiles Joseph, Esther and Daniel.

Exiles feel like a "motherless child," that is, abandoned, rootless, vulnerable, orphaned. The exiles in Babylon felt a deep grief about the loss of their nation and the humiliation of their God. Expressing such sadness is a good and healthy thing (that's what the book of Lamentations is all about), but the temptation of the exile is to embrace a narrow way of thinking that can't imagine you can live out your identity on foreign soil. When exiles give in to that temptation they find themselves in a ghetto mentality, hunkering down and resisting the prevailing culture. What exiles yearn for is an invitation to live, as Walter Brueggemann describes it, "freely, dangerously, and tenaciously in a world where faith does not have its own way."[1] And here lies the root of the problem of the church today. Victimized by nostalgia and buffeted by fear, the church is focused too much on merely holding the small plot of ground it currently occupies to confidently reimagine a robust future. The result is a retreat into some fundamentalist us-versus-them model, rather than "an endlessly cunning, risky process of negotiation."[2]

When God does start stirring up new things, we need to respond quickly and courageously. At a time when the church is required to be adaptive and fearless, the tendency has been the opposite, to retreat into inflexibility and fear. Many churches have tended to swing between needing to conquer and control their situation or withdrawing from it completely. The story we told in the previous chapter about the street pastors' work in Manly is an example of a middle way. None of us in Manly would ever have imagined running a street chaplaincy ministry. Its creation emerged due to our responsive flexibility. We needed to abandon our much-loved traditions of running events and agree to enter, like salt and light, into the brokenness of our neighborhood. This leads us to the fourth midwifery practice we want to commend.

MIDWIFE PRACTICE #4: BEING FLEXIBLE AND FEARLESS

The delicate work of a midwife requires an openness to enter fully into a situation without dominating it. And it isn't easy. Even in overseas missionary communities, where incarnational engagement has a high value, you can see the slide toward withdrawal. I (Michael) once spent some time in a missionary compound (that's what it was referred to) just outside Nairobi. Formerly the Brackenridge country club, a getaway for the British colonial rulers of Kenya, the missionaries had converted the main building, including a grand Tudor-style banquet hall, into a conference center and built missionary housing, a chapel and a training institute on the grounds. Brackenridge is set majestically high on a green hill, surrounded by lush tea plantations and separated from the nearby villages by high security fencing. The manicured lawns and gardens and the decorated homes of the (mainly) American missionaries made it feel like a little slice of suburban Texas in the middle of Africa. And yet, there would be little doubt that all the American inhabitants of that compound traveled to Africa with a strong sense of wanting to live among the people to whom God had sent them.

I (Christiana) know the subtleties and complexities of this impulse only too well. I was raised in a Christian missionary community in Tokyo, Japan, where I observed my parents and their fellow missionaries giving their lives to love the Japanese people and to introduce them to Jesus. From my vantage point, their evangelistic strategies were genuine and heartfelt. I witnessed the fruit of their everyday goodness and kindness resulting in real life change. As one can imagine, however, there were many layers of cultural distance between us and our Japanese neighbors—differences of customs, language, belief systems and values. It was a weighty challenge for my parents and others to actively pursue our Japanese neighbors not simply as ones we came to serve but also as ones to share life and mutual friendship.

It is common in these kinds of contexts to develop an "us-and-them" paradigm. Us internationals and those who are Japanese. Us living with temporary immigrant visas and those native to the country. Us Christians, the saved ones, and those who need God.

This polarizing paradigm is a universal phenomenon. We naturally differentiate, creating separations and sometimes hierarchies. Anyone who's lived internationally knows firsthand the sting of culture shock and disorientation. Most of the time, however, in preparation for international living there is at least a degree of work put into developing a skill for enculturation in order to integrate with optimum ease and help minimize the strain of adaptation.

The us-and-them mentality, however, is not just reserved for crosscultural encounters but also impacts the way in which we live within our home cultures. As followers of Jesus, we would do well to develop enculturation skills that not only help us integrate in our own societies but also awaken us to the universal realities of the human experience, of which we are an inseparable part.

When it comes to belief systems or religion, dualistic thinking in this way is certainly dicey. It is understandable to differentiate ourselves from those who do not believe what we believe. At some levels, this kind of clarity is helpful and healthy. Connecting with others who share our values and beliefs is strengthening and provides an important sense of belonging. Yet often the dissociations we as Christians tend to make from those whose faith persuasions differ from our own comes with a level of ego that is most definitely not helpful nor healthy for anyone involved. We believe that differentiating ourselves as "Christians" and "non-Christians" to the point where we no longer recognize our common humanity is inimical to the very heart of God for humankind. Our separation debilitates our ability to sincerely love and be loved in the way that

Jesus inaugurated. And such separation is nearly always the result of fear. Following God into mission can't lead to an us-and-them mentality. We need to enter fully into the societies in which God has placed us and seek to be as adaptable and daring as possible.

There are not many jobs that require as much adaptability as a midwife. Every birth is different. Every laboring mother will respond slightly differently to her situation. No delivery room is exactly the same, and midwives learn quickly to respond to changes in any particular birth. The role of the midwife is to usher a mother and baby through their experience with sensitivity and strength. This process requires flexibility at every turn of the plot. Things will never go as planned. The midwife learns to see deviation as a part of the mysterious unknown unfolding before her. Likewise, we must follow the impulse of the Spirit, embracing the unexpected and anticipating the uncommon.

Leaders of minority communities are pioneering what it looks like to give back to the neighborhood, especially those that are under-resourced and written off. These leaders are community activators who've come from a long heritage of grassroots organizing, community formation, and church expressions from the ground up, engaging social issues with faithfulness and resilience. They know how to be flexible and fearless.

One such leader is Reesheda Graham-Washington. After leaving home for graduate studies, she returned to her community to teach at her old school, following her calling to contribute to the betterment of education in her city of Berwyn, an urban community in the greater Chicago area. She rose through the ranks to become a school principal and then a regional administrator. These days, Graham-Washington is the executive director of Communities First Association, a faith-based organization committed to community transformation through the multiplication of leaders trained in asset-based community development. Her latest entrepreneurial venture is L!VE Cafe, a for-profit coffee house business with the stated vision of contributing to the community by fanning the flame of social innovation and enterprise, inspiring people toward courageous, authentic and abundant living. Graham-Washington is a licensed minister in the Evangelical Covenant Church and has a gracious and enlivening vision for neighborhood churches in urban contexts. Her life's work is an inspiration and an example of creatively attending to God in the birth of the new creation.

As we referenced earlier, Jesus explicitly describes the Spirit as the one who gives birth to the spiritual life. The Greek word "spirit" used here is interchangeable with the word "wind." It implies an ever-present, uncontainable movement. Just after declaring the Spirit as the one who gives birth, Jesus goes on to say, "So don't be surprised when I say, 'You must be born again.' The wind blows wherever it wants. Just as you can hear the wind but can't tell where it comes from or where it is going, so you can't explain how people are born of the Spirit" (Jn 3:7-8 NLT).

In the process of birthing new communities, churches and transformative structures, the Spirit, like the wind, will move in ways we cannot anticipate. We need to remain in step with what the Spirit is birthing around us. In management theory this is sometimes called adaptive leadership. It was developed from more than thirty years of research at Harvard University by Ronald Heifetz and Marty Linsky. Essentially, adaptive leadership is defined as "an approach that helps individuals and organizations adapt to challenging environments by being able, both individually and collectively, to take on the gradual but meaningful process of change to the status quo."[3]

One of the key aspects of Heifetz and Linsky's model is the need for leaders to determine which practices are precious and which are expendable. They claim that it is only when you realize what your organization's essential aspirations are that you can be adaptable enough to abandon the expendable practices and innovate with new approaches. Adaptive leaders have become adept at diagnosing the precious, interrupting the expendable and innovating with the better.

It can sound like corporate-speak, but we think it's a useful framework. Many church leaders struggle to adapt. Even the ones who think they are adaptable can be enslaved to traditional categories. The key to the theory of adaptive leadership is figuring out what's precious and what's expendable. This doesn't mean we adapt uncritically to our circumstances. Far from it. We are forced to enter deeply into the work of examining what is precious and nonnegotiable about the reign of God and our place in it. Church leaders must help their congregations to see the disconnect between what it is and what it ought to be, and then learn and adapt accordingly in ways that honor its values and history.

As we've noted, beginning with prefabricated models of mission and ministry doesn't help. Articulating to the congregation where they ought to be going and trying to motivate them to go there is a tough gig. But bringing a congregation together and equipping them to listen to their neighborhood, release their agendas, shape their environments, hold the space and trust God can be catalytic. In other words, instead of saying, "Here's what we should be doing," leaders need to frame it as, "Here's who we should be becoming." Rather than insisting on the expendable, insist on the precious and allow the congregation to discuss it and pray about it. You'll be amazed by two things that happen. First, much better ideas will emerge, and second, much more responsibility will be taken for implementing them. Adaptive leaders see their responsibility as catalysts who are more concerned with asking the right questions than with giving the "right" strategies.

Adaptive missional leaders have biblically-shaped convictions regarding the mission of God, and they stay the church's hand in that direction. But the expendable, temporary, immediate models of achieving those goals are always up for negotiation. Like an adaptable midwife, we are to remain a stable, calm presence, assessing the situation, asking the right questions, trusting the process and participating in the things God is doing.

But adaptive missional leadership also involves being flexible when things don't go according to our preconceived expectations. Some of our greatest setbacks or perceived failures can be the essential ingredient for something profoundly mysterious and healing to come into being. We've all been there—that place in time when what we hoped and dreamed for seemed to crumble before our very eyes. Sometimes the thing we thought we wanted, or needed, wasn't best for us. The humbling path of defeat can be the doorway to our greatest growth. And life is more about growth than success because successes are a distant, dissolving memory while growth is an ongoing process into our future.

Our experiences of perceived failure become parables for what it looks like to trust God's process of grace in our lives, even when things don't go as we planned, when we don't get what we want or when we weather defeat. In the process of labor, often the methods used for coping with pain or fostering labor progression can have the opposite effect from what we hoped. Labor stalls, or the baby's position isn't optimum for a smooth delivery. Instead of freaking out, digging our heels in or considering these setbacks as useless, the midwife adapts and troubleshoots. And sometimes trying what shouldn't work becomes the pathway to what is actually needed.

As we lead churches and communities of faith or organizations for transformation we will always come up against our own defeats and inadequacies—those times when we don't see as much social change as we'd like to, when that person we've been walking with makes an unhealthy life choice or relapses, when our great ideas dissolve and when we can't get enough people to join our latest project. Sometimes these same disappointments become opportunities to be led by the wisdom and foreknowledge of God, who sees far beyond our ideals. And through it all, we are made better, stronger, more honest and more dependent on the sovereignty of God's goodness. As Eckhart Tolle says, "Some changes may look negative on the surface but you will soon realize that space is being created in your life for something new to emerge."[4]

Darren and Pam Prince serve with InnerCHANGE in the East End of London, England. Before planting their lives in the United Kingdom, they worked for nearly ten years in the heart of San Francisco's Mission District, where they lived among the homeless runaway population. They began with a vision to join God's work of restoration as they befriended the often forgotten and overlooked of their city. This vision for restorative justice was hard to see in the everyday, nitty-gritty of their work, yet they faithfully gave their lives to embody the gospel of Jesus in daily, tangible ways. Darren reflects on the sometimes discouraging nature of inevitable mistakes we make as we move toward the vision that God gives us:

> Some of our biggest mistakes have been with dear people for whom we wanted the best but sometimes were only able to give simplistic, naive or incomplete responses to their deepest problems. In our early days of helping people who were living on the streets, we would mistakenly ask them to join in on our way of life and ministry prematurely. In InnerCHANGE we have a commitment to live as communities of incarnational mission wherever God calls us. But there were times when inviting our street friends to join in was something neither they nor we were ready for, leading to hurt feelings and harmed friendships along the way. Things changed as we learned to listen better to the real needs of those we knew from the streets—including their own hopes and dreams for

themselves: finding employment, connecting to a local church, moving further into health and sobriety by facing into their past addictions and trauma.

With time, some of these friends became our housemates and we learned the give-and-take of authentic community as people struggling together on the margins. We formed patterns of mutual formation and shared discipleship: new rhythms which were accessible to all of us. We learned to have patience with each other coming from both ends of cultural-economic adjustment. And we developed authentic ways of partnering together for the common good. I'm not sure we could have reached these important learnings without accepting our failures along the way.[5]

Embracing the unknown means accepting our failures as an integral part of any ministry vision. Our deficiencies can be the key stimulus for our greatest growth and our most fruitful work. The Spirit is nurturing something out of the soil of our mistakes. The Spirit is concerned about health and grace and wholeness. There is always a unique birth story at play, a story like no other. Adaptation means accepting what we don't know and what we can't do in order to embrace the needed process. It is accepting our shortcomings and our failures to walk the path of transformation with enduring patience and enlivening hope.

MIDWIFE PRACTICE #5: LIVING OUT A NEW NARRATIVE

What would happen if churches could enter fully into their neighborhoods and become the influential presence we talked about earlier? What if church leaders could suspend all judgments, release their agendas and take seriously the space into which they have entered? What if adaptive missional leaders could identify what is essential and precious and renegotiate absolutely everything else? What would happen next? Surely, then and only then can we live out a new narrative, an alternative plot to the prevailing storyline of the surrounding culture. As we said, in adaptive leadership you need to diagnose, interrupt and innovate to create the opportunities that match your church's missional aspirations. Once you've developed and tested "next" practices you need to live them out.

We've rarely met a midwife who is argumentative. Instead of disputing their values and perspectives with their words, midwives simply choose to live out another story. They often take the route of modeling an alternative way rather than simply defending their perspective with rhetoric. Midwives usually know the global statistics of successful birth support. They've often been educated to understand varied forms of obstetric care. They understand human physiology and psychology, and they've rigorously studied the tools available in the birth process to assist in any unexpected complication. When birthing mothers and their partners are falling apart or panicking, midwives remain calm and focused, guiding them toward the care they need. They live out the alternative reality to which they are inviting their patients.

You might not find people in your context as flustered or unnerved as those in a delivery room, but you shouldn't assume they are any less at home with their circumstances. In her marvelous book on the current malaise of modern life, Ann Morisy refers to society as "bothered and bewildered."[6] Even more scathing is writer Richard Matheson, who described contemporary life as monotonous, long-suffering and tedious:

> We've forgotten much. How to struggle, how to rise to dizzy
> heights and sink to unparalleled depths. We no longer aspire
> to anything. Even the finer shades of despair are lost to us.
> We've ceased to be runners. We plod from structure to

conveyance to employment and back again. We live within the boundaries that science has determined for us. The measuring stick is short and sweet. The full gamut of life is a brief, shadowy continuum that runs from gray to more gray. The rainbow is bleached. We hardly know how to doubt anymore.[7]

People are looking for alternatives to the grayness of modern life. Where will they find them? How wonderful it would be if they found the church as the source of real hope in such troubling times, a living, breathing sign of the narrative of God's promised peace and redemption.

Some of the most prophetically charged, world-changing movements throughout history were catalyzed, not by charismatic leaders taking the world by force, but by small groups of faithful people on the fringe of society who chose to embody an alternative story to that of the prevailing culture around them. The Celtic revival of Europe in the seventh century comes to mind here, as do the monastic movements of the medieval period. Much later, the Welsh revivals and the Azusa Street revival were noted for being spread by poor, untrained Welsh miners-turned-evangelists or poor urban Angelinos. More recently, the world has seen the growth of the South Korean church fueled by small groups led by women, and the emergence of the lay-led church planting movements of South and Latin America.

We have had the privilege of observing adaptive missional leaders and their communities at work in varied places around the world, in big churches, small churches and house churches; neighborhood church communities made up of hipsters, quirks and misfits; traditional, progressive, liberal and conservative. We're fascinated by each of these approaches to living as communities of faith. We're also fascinated by the beautiful people who lead these churches. They are contributing to a new narrative.

Mark and Nadine Reichman are leaders of a unique faith community in Karlsruhe, Germany, pioneering an expression of the church that we find refreshing and provocative. Mark, Nadine and their two boys are part of Mateno, an intentional community of Jesus followers who are living out their faith in simple and enduring ways that are changing the world around them.

After several years of living in the downtown Karlsruhe area of Southwest Germany and starting a popular concert venue for big name European artists, a small band of people separated from the wider community and moved up the hill into a building that was formerly a convent birthed out of the Schoenstatt Movement in the early 1900s. This Catholic movement was centered on the love of God with an emphasis on developing the unique calling of each person in the body of Christ. Mateno beautifully articulates that they "continue the story that God is writing" by living as an intentional community, learning to love one another and extend the love they've been given as they help others discover their unique calling and contribution in God's world. These folks have a strong expression of radical hospitality, agricultural sustainability and creation care, contemplative spirituality, and cultivation of justice and stewardship in their everyday choices. They host art and music events as well as trainings and gatherings for other faith leaders in the region who desire to see the church expressed in fresh and innovative ways in their own European contexts. Mark is now the regional representative of Forge Europe, coming alongside leaders for the church of tomorrow.

As we stated earlier, joining what the Spirit is birthing means living a new narrative in contrast to that of the pervading culture, be that the Christian culture or broader culture. In a post-Christian context such as Germany, what the Reichmans and their community are creating is unconventional and off the beaten path. They are laying new ground by embodying an alternative reality and ushering in what the Spirit of God is birthing in their world.

Another story illustrating the practice of living out a new narrative within the culture comes from Tim and Mary Dickau, whose lives have had a ripple effect in spreading God's goodness in Grandview-Woodlands, Vancouver, British Columbia. Tim and Mary have pastored Grandview Calvary Baptist Church in their neighborhood for over twenty-five years, embodying the wisdom that comes from long, faithful incarnational mission.

In the early years of their church plant, the Dickaus encouraged and challenged members who lived outside the neighborhood to relocate into the Grandview area and commit to investing in the well-being of their place together. They had no idea what this kind of challenge would produce. As the church community began to take this challenge seriously, more than 75 percent of the members lived within walking proximity to the church building. Among many other initiatives, they developed a creative vision to start a series of hospitality homes, which eventually became known as the Salsbury Community Society. Tim describes the process of forming these communities in his book, *Plunging into the Kingdom Way.*

> The establishment of these houses thrust us to root in the Grandview-Woodlands neighborhood even further as we began to model a way of life together that many people would be drawn into and others would seek to imitate. In these houses, people chose to live together for varying reasons such as economic need, loneliness, support to overcome addictions, help in the struggle with mental illness or support for adapting to a new country [specifically with refugees].[8]

As they have participated in social, economic and governmental matters, championing peace and justice in their place, Grandview Calvary Baptist Church continues to stimulate change at systemic levels. As the church community became more and more aware of their neighbors' needs they eventually started an array of initiatives to support their flourishing—tutoring for children, leadership development for teens, support for single mothers, shelter for their street population, social enterprises for people with barriers to employment and affordable community housing, to name a few. And their involvement has not gone unnoticed. The local community health coordinator remarked that Grandview Calvary Baptist Church is one of the major city partners in the community well-being. This kind of acknowledgment speaks volumes to the new narrative of God's redemption that this church is pioneering together.

Another story in particular comes to mind as we conceptualize what it can look like to contribute to a new narrative in our context beyond the constructs of church-sponsored events. It concerns Rebecca Chase and Jen Byard and the establishment of Makers Arcade.

In 2014, Rebecca and Jen cofounded Makers Arcade, a locally curated creative arts fair in urban San Diego.[9] Both Jesus followers and local artisans themselves, they were passionate about building community in their city by highlighting local craft and creative entrepreneurism. The sheer number of those who attended their first Makers Arcade experience was staggering. The event appealed to a wide range of San Diegoians from all over the county with a concentration from the urban center and surrounding neighborhoods. Folks came out not only to shop for local inventions and creations but also to experience the whole atmosphere of the event.

With everything from product exhibits, décor and architected lounge spaces to craft cocktails and live music from local bands, Makers Arcade is an all-out fantastic, party-like experience. Every last detail is locally run, locally fueled and locally attended. For their fourth biannual event, an estimated four-thousand-plus San Diegoians came to experience what the occasion had to offer.

I (Christiana) met a young woman at one of the events who commented, "This event isn't just an expression of San Diego creative energy, it's actually fashioning our creative culture." This woman had just moved back to San Diego after being away for three years. She was amazed by the steep shift of creative culture she observed, crediting Makers Arcade as one of the contributing catalysts.

The Makers Arcade story is a beautiful glimpse into something the Spirit is birthing in the creative community of San Diego. The event continues to expand and deepen, and the relational bonds are the threads of true community with unbelievable potential for spiritual awakening and social change in the enlightened way of Jesus. It is a San Diego cultural expression, and interwoven from corner to corner, Jesus followers are present and participating and creating.

To be clear, we share this story to illustrate a way in which followers of Jesus can together join in on what God is birthing in the world. Many of us are familiar with a way of joining God that involves putting on church events or ministry projects. Often we do this with our church logo visibly front and center. Some of these church-sponsored events wither quickly while others feel successful but with limited impact on the surrounding culture. Putting on church events is one way of engaging culture and certainly a viable way of affecting a city. But as we shift our questions away from, "How can our church be known?" to, "What does the world really need?" and act accordingly, the tide of culture could take a dramatic turn. God is inviting the church to live a new narrative in the world, using our gifts and passions to bring people together and creatively contend for global equity in every sector of society, infusing the values of the kingdom of God . . . everywhere.

So what if we flipped this whole church event thing around and stopped asking the question, "How can we put on a special event to draw people into relationship with us or our church as an expression of the goodness of God?" and instead asked, "What is God doing in the world to connect people, meet needs and express goodness, and how can we join in?" We must adapt to the needs and desires around us. Then we join God not as a promo for our church but as an expression of our life values, informed by Christ. Our mission no longer becomes about our particular brand of church but about the impulse of God's creative love, already in motion, already birthing something. It means releasing our agendas, stepping into the unknown, adapting to every change, holding the space and instituting a new narrative. It could be revolutionary.

7 HOW TO REALLY CHANGE THE WORLD

*Christ has no body now but yours. No hands,
no feet on earth but yours. Yours are the eyes
through which he looks compassion on this world.
Yours are the feet with which he walks to do good.
Yours are the hands through which he blesses all
the world. Yours are the hands, yours are the feet,
yours are the eyes, you are his body.
Christ has no body now on earth but yours.*

SAINT TERESA OF ÁVILA

There has been a plethora of books in recent years about how Christians can change the world. Many of them urge us to engage society, mobilize our forces and win the culture wars. But let's face it, whenever the church tries to rule the world it never goes well for us. Indeed, we would suggest most of the criticisms leveled at the church by its detractors relate to the church's abuse of temporal power. It's nice to imagine the church as an ancient remedy that brings healing and repair to a diseased system, but increasingly, people have spoken of the church more in terms of a virus than a tonic.

Journalist Christopher Hitchens wasn't one to pull punches. In his 2007 book *God Is Not Great: How Religion Poisons Everything*, he said, "Violent, irrational, intolerant, allied to racism and tribalism and bigotry, invested in ignorance and hostile to free inquiry, contemptuous of women and coercive toward children: organized religion ought to have a great deal on its conscience."[1] For Hitchens, Christianity is responsible for widespread intolerance, the Inquisition, the Crusades, slavery and a litany of wickedness.

Adopting this same line is John Loftus, a former Christian minister and now an atheist. In 2014, he published the anthology *Christianity Is Not Great*, in which a group of scholars focused on what they perceived to be the damage done by the church throughout history covering everything from the Crusades, the Spanish Inquisition and witch hunts to bogus faith healing. Loftus concludes, "The Christian faith can be empirically tested by the amount of harm it has done and continues to do in our world. Jesus reportedly said: 'By their fruits ye shall know them' (Matthew 7:20). When we evaluate the fruits of Christianity, the result is that it fails miserably."[2]

We've all had conversations with antagonistic non-Christians who remind us of the Inquisition, the number of incidents of sexual abuse by clergy, particularly in the Catholic Church, the belittling and condemnatory treatment of women and the LGBTQ community, and the offensive behavior and statements of Westboro Baptist Church in Kansas.

And often all we can do is take it on the chin and admit that our brothers and sisters (though usually our brothers) have not represented the teachings of Jesus very well. If all this was the sum total of Christianity's contribution to society, it would be reasonable to ask what Christianity ever did for us. But, of course, that's only half the story (maybe much less than half). Whenever we hear an atheist attacking the poisonous nature of Christianity we're reminded of that scene in *Monty Python's Life of Brian*, where John Cleese asks the People's Liberation Front of Judea, "What have the Romans ever done for us?" When the members of his audience start listing things like sanitation, medicine, education, wine, public order, irrigation, roads, a fresh water system, public health and peace, he deadpans, "What have the Romans ever done for us except sanitation, medicine, education . . . ?"[3] The fact is that Christianity has altered European culture, indeed Western society as a whole, for the better in extraordinary ways.

WHAT HAVE THE CHRISTIANS EVER DONE FOR US?

Seeking to counter all this bad news, British scholar Jonathan Hill wrote *What Has Christianity Ever Done for Us?*, an exploration of the positive contributions the faith has made to culture and thought, the arts, education, politics and society. It includes intriguing stuff like the reason why we seal wine bottles with cork (the monk Dom Pérignon came up with the idea), where musical notation came from (another monk, Guido dÁrezzo), how universities got their start (Pope Gregory kicked things off) and why the world's first fully literate society wasn't in Europe, Asia or North America (it was Armenia, thanks to the enterprising work of a missionary with the impressive name Mesrob Mashtots).

But more significantly, Hill also documents the considerable impact Christianity has had on education, health care, literacy, law and order, orphan care and social justice. Christianity, Hill argues, gave us the European languages as we know them, our calendar, our moral framework and more. Christians have contributed a huge amount to art, literature, music, architecture, politics and the sciences. Hill's work is not ignorant of the harm done by Christians throughout history. He acknowledges that Christians contributed to the system of slavery, while also reminding us it was believers like William Wilberforce who ended it. He mentions that while Christians were at the forefront of the anti-apartheid and the civil rights movements, there were also Christians in the Dutch Reformed Church of South Africa and the Southern Baptist Convention that opposed them. For every Christian bigot, racist or hypocrite, Hill can counter with an Albrecht Ritschl, a Walter Rauschenbusch, a Martin Luther King or a Dorothy Day. Ultimately, he concludes,

> Christianity has influenced the modern world in a huge number of ways. Sometimes it has done so as the dominant ideology. Literacy and education in the West, for example, owe a great debt to the Christian rule of people such as Justinian and Charlemagne. But sometimes it has done so from a position of relative weakness—such as the political activism of people such as Helder Camara or Janani Luwum. . . . While being in authority gives the church the means to act for the good, often being out of authority gives it more of a motivation.[4]

And there's the point. When the church has exercised temporal power it has had mixed results, both good and evil. But when the church operates without such power its motivation for change is far greater. And we shouldn't be surprised by this. Jesus described the kingdom of God not like an army but like a seed. His description of the world God is giving birth to as a mustard seed was intriguing and obviously well chosen. The mustard seed is, as Jesus describes it, a tiny seed. But it grows into a very unruly tree. New Testament scholar Ben Witherington notes that Jesus could have chosen a different tree for the parable, one that grows tall and straight like a cedar, for example, if his point was merely about size. But in choosing a plant that is both fast-growing and self-germinating (more like a malignant weed than a majestic tree), Jesus adds greater complexity to his metaphor. The mustard tree is an annoying tree with a deep and widespread root system. In fact, uprooting a mature mustard tree is a dreadful business. As Witherington says, referring to the growth of the church, "Though the dominion appeared small like a seed during Jesus' ministry, it would inexorably grow into something large and firmly rooted, which some would find shelter in and others would find obnoxious and try to root out."[5] The followers of Jesus are at our best when we adopt the more subversive and scandalous role of the mustard shrub than we do when trying to reach for the skies like a cedar.

Like an obnoxious weed, the people of God have sent roots out throughout the world, usually shaping history in a subversive way. Christianity has given shape and direction to European culture and, subsequently, to many of the Western cultures that emerged from it, including the United States. Many of our practices, traditions, norms, customs and taboos have their roots in Christianity. We value forgiveness, not vengeance; love and tolerance, not extremism (even if we don't always live them out perfectly). We accept fundamentally that all humans are equal and of value, and that we need to respect all living creatures, not merely as for my benefit. From Protestant culture we have imbibed a very strong sense of independence and rebellion, of choosing to act on our own fate rather than accepting it, being responsible for our own actions and never blindly following a hierarchy or status quo. We cannot admire any religion or sect that degrades and enslaves women or abuses animals. We don't believe in ghosts or magic, even though we know there are many things we do not understand about the way the world and life work. We are curious about the world and feel in awe of it. We embrace science and proof and investigation, but understand that science has no answers about the nature of existence, spirituality or morality. We embrace nature and feel a spiritual connection to it. In all these things, we act differently from someone brought up in a culture of Hinduism, Islam, Judaism, Buddhism or spirit animism. We got all that from the creeping, grassroots influence of Christianity.

These things weren't legislated. They were adopted from the roots up. So, while it might be true that churches in the West today feel metaphorically exiled from society, where greater humility and circumspection is required of the church, we cannot back away from our vocation of honoring God, loving our neighbors, serving the common good and pursuing God's restorative purposes over all of life. And when we do those things we alter culture from the bottom up.

A THEORY OF SOCIAL CHANGE

As we've pointed out, we fear that the emphasis on church planting (often rootless churches) and political lobbying hasn't yielded the kind of culture change the church desires. We conclude that if *all* a church does is to start a Sunday morning worship service, we won't see the kind of social reverberations we've talked about. If, however, the community of Christ followers understands themselves, like a mustard tree, as an essential element inserted into the very *warp and woof* of their society, the effect cannot help but be felt.

Most people don't use the expression warp and woof any more. It's from weaving, where a fabric is comprised of the warp—the threads that run lengthwise—and the woof—the threads that run across. There's a reference to it in Leviticus 13, which contains a lengthy discussion about mildewed clothing as well as Hebrew regulations for infectious skin diseases (including colorful descriptions of spots and boils and rashes). We won't blame you if you've missed that chapter. In brief, the law states that if an item of clothing has become mildewed—whether in warp or in woof—it is to be burned. That is to say, once a contaminant gets into the warp and woof it can't be removed— it's in the very essence of the fabric. Societies are like fabric. They are comprised of tight-knit networks of interlocking parts. For the church to enter into a society it must do so in every part of its constitution, committed to goodness everywhere. Below, this is depicted as a series of stackable containers, each fitting within the others:

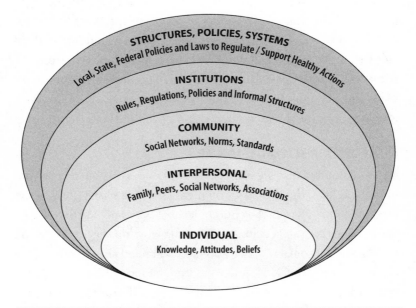

Figure 7.1. Levels of influence in the Social Ecological Model[6]

As we mentioned earlier, the church has focused its attention on the smallest and the largest of these stackable containers—on individual transformation (evangelism) and on political outcomes—without recognizing the importance of all five levels of society. If we are to take our role as God's representatives seriously we need to note that our job of entering society incarnationally—suspending our agendas, holding space and living a new narrative—should function at every one of these levels.

Emory University has developed a theory of social change that takes all five of these echelons of society into account:

1. Individual change. The Emory model makes clear that for social change to occur there needs to be the transformation of individuals and an alignment of their beliefs and practices. This is evidenced in two key ways—awareness of self and empathy with others. If we apply the theory to the church, it basically means that Christians need to develop an increasing awareness of their own beliefs, values and abilities, as well as an increasing ability to understand and appreciate the beliefs, life experiences and values of others. Take the civil rights movement in the 1960s as an example. Activists were schooled thoroughly in their own beliefs about human dignity and political and social equity, as well as the value they placed on nonviolence, *and* they learned to understand the mentality of those who opposed them. It was a profoundly important part of the movement. If the church is to change culture then we need to recruit more people to this cause (evangelism) as well as train our current members in self-awareness and empathy toward others, not demonizing or caricaturing others, but understanding their opposition to the church's values.

2. Interpersonal change. The Emory Social Change Model also values the necessity of learning the principles and practices of peer-to-peer influence. This can only occur when the change agents (the church, for our discussion) have developed a high level of congruence between their own values and their actions (integrity). Having aligned these things, the individual then looks to implement such an integrated life among others. In short, when people live with congruence between their actions and values, and have empathy for others, they have significant interpersonal impact. They are aware of their own values and attitudes, and have committed to living a life of purpose that aligns with those values in the context of family, peers and other social networks. They are highly influential people.

3. Community change. The third dimension to Emory's model is an emphasis on collaboration and problem solving—learning the ability to work cooperatively and effectively with others in ways that empower people, valuing their gifts and contributions. People can only learn to truly cooperate and problem solve when they have an appreciation for differences and are able to empathize with those with whom they interact. According to the Emory approach, community change is impossible without the two prior steps, because without self-awareness, empathy and congruence, there is little likelihood of genuine collaboration. Sadly, many Christian leaders see collaboration as compromise. They are happy to call their members to self-awareness, empathy and congruence, but are resistant to the kind of trusting and empowering partnership that is necessary with those with whom they disagree theologically or morally.

4. Institutional change. Changing the regulations, policies and even the informal structures of our institutions requires a significant commitment to action—a kind of call to arms, not to storm the barricades, but to commit to the painstaking process of revision and change. Developing the motivation to bring change, fostering buy-in and support, and becoming actively involved in individual and collaborative efforts to bring about social change requires serious commitment. Leaders in this process have to understand the diversity of thought of their followers in order to inspire and motivate them. They also need to continually emphasize the commonality of purpose, working together with shared aims and values. Social change is best achieved when the majority of the members of a society or community share in the vision and actively participate in realizing it.

5. Societal change. Widespread societal change is only achieved through the ethical engagement and citizenship of the change agents. According to Emory, for this to occur, the church needs to "promote positive civic engagement and social responsibility with an ethic of service and a concern for justice."[7] The Emory Social Change Model's core value is citizenship, "a process whereby the individual and the collaborative group become responsibly connected to the community and the society through their leadership toward whatever social change is required."[8] In other words, it's the goal of all good citizens to contribute toward positive change in society. This is at the very center of Emory's entire model. The Emory model says, "Citizenship thus acknowledges the interdependence of all who are involved in or affected by these efforts. It recognizes that the common purpose of the group must incorporate a sense of concern for the rights and welfare of all those who might be affected by the group's efforts. Good citizenship thus recognizes that effective democracy involves individual responsibility as well as individual rights. This focus on citizenship and change means improving the status quo, creating a better world, and demonstrating a comfort with transition and ambiguity in the change process."[9]

The Emory model can be summarized with the following series of C words—consciousness of self (including empathy), congruence, commitment, collaboration, common purpose and citizenship. It is shown on the earlier diagram here:

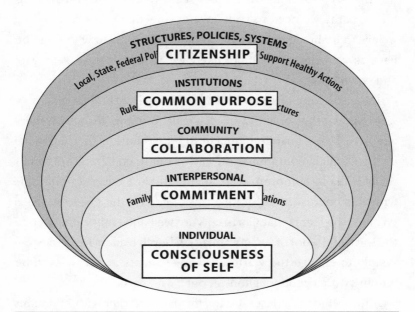

Figure 7.2. The Emory Social Change Model

For the most part the church has been better at the lower levels—
encouraging personal self-awareness, congruence and commitment—than the broader levels of emphasizing collaboration,
commonality with others and good citizenship. In saying that, it's
good to focus on the interpersonal and individual tiers. Fostering
healthy individual self-knowledge, self-love and gut-level vulnerability is the bedrock of transformational growth and these are the
building blocks for true community. But to catalyze social change
there needs to be more work done on the three higher tiers in this
diagram. And that means equipping all Christians to see collaboration, commonality and citizenship as legitimate expressions of
their faith in Christ.

EMBRACING COLLABORATION AND COMMONALITY

It is this very act of growing in our self-awareness that births in us
the empathy we need to truly love our neighbor. The less willing
we are to embrace our shared humanity with those who don't believe as we believe, the more likely we are to separate, segregate
and condemn.

The inclination of some Christians to separate and go their own
way impedes the possibility of such collaboration. We believe there
needs to be an abandonment of any assumption that all social
contact equals contamination and genuine collaboration necessarily leads to compromise. The church can't afford to continue
with this impulse to separate and still call on the need for social
change. The fact is that Christians are well and truly embedded in
the warp and woof of society already. Church leaders need to equip
people to engage the world as change agents at every level, beginning with a good long look at our own hearts.

If the followers of Jesus are to effectively partner with him in his
empire-shattering, culture-changing work we must abandon our

impulse to separate from the society we wish to influence. As we've outlined so far, altering culture involves the following commitments:

- Enter society as a potentially disruptive presence.
- Suspend prefabricated agendas and follow the opportunities as God presents them.
- Hold the space in which God is working by taking the context very seriously.
- Remain flexible and adaptable, following the cues of the Spirit.
- Live out a viable and appealing alternative reality to the world around us.

Now we wish to add a sixth commitment: embrace the necessary collaboration to affect change in every level of society.

Our incarnational call as followers of Christ necessitates that we love with a sincerity that draws us closer to those who are different from us, honors that divine spark in every human soul and acknowledges that God's love binds us together. This kind of love will change the world as we know it. It is a love that is best embodied in the way of Jesus; a love that makes it possible for us to embrace the kind of collaboration with our neighbors that is necessary for meaningful cultural change.

It is quite possible to collaborate at this level without compromising our convictions as Christ followers. In fact, staying true to our faith and acknowledging our differences is crucial in effective partnerships. We will lose ourselves in the process if we think that the way of the chameleon is best. It is simply not so. Staying genuine and honest to our convictions is vital for authentic relationship. When we know who we are and we are willing to agree to disagree with others, we fashion a space for real collaboration. And it is very likely that we will actually learn a thing or two along the way!

A Southern California church took this challenge to heart as they intentionally sought to partner with their neighbors of differing religions. Their church building was situated next to a mosque, and instead of building hedges to protect themselves, they built relationships to nurture love and partner together for the good of their city. Building trusted relationships took time. Church staff visited the mosque to learn more about Islam and invited the imam and his family to share their stories with the rest of their church congregation. They started playing pickup soccer with each other and attending each other's birthday parties and special events. These kinds of regular relationship-building engagements led to a fruitful process of what it might look like to dream together for how they could bless their city.

Interfaith dialogues and enterprises are popping up all over the world. We've seen Christian leaders, rabbis and imams working together to produce prophetic initiatives for peace and justice in volatile situations like the Israel and Palestine conflict. We've witnessed business executives, church leaders and social entrepreneurs sitting around a table discussing the plight of the homeless and houseless community in their urban center, together seeking to create structures for a more humane future. Denominational representatives have assembled interfaith leaders in Africa who desire to stimulate systemic change as they address the problem of contaminated water sources that directly affect local farm owners and community health. The collaborative way of Jesus guides us toward a joint effort to usher in the world God envisions.

KEY INDICATORS OF A CHANGED CITY

It seems as though churches are very focused on key indicators and modes of measurement. There's been plenty of criticism that churches only measure attendance and finances. At least they're easy things to count. But Ed Stetzer says (rather colorfully), "We must start counting more than baptisms, butts, and bucks!"[10] Merely making tallies of the number of members and the size of the offering means churches focus unduly on attracting new members and increasing tithing. We're not opposed to counting people per se. After all, when our families take outings we count that all the kids are in the car for the journey home. We're just concerned that if that's *all* the church counts it betrays a huge Sunday focus. As Reggie McNeal says, what is needed is "a shift in what counts and is counted."[11]

And yet, when it's pointed out that only counting nickels, noses and numbers means the church is turning in on itself and losing its interest in changing society, many pastors are stumped as to the alternative. Chicago pastor Dave Ferguson, author of *Keeping Score*, points out, "It is my observation that for most church leaders, it is a mystery about what really counts, what we should count and how do we get points on the board for the mission."[12] So what do churches committed to altering society actually count to determine how well they're achieving their goals?

Montreal-based urban missionary Glenn Smith has developed a framework for thinking about how to engage in social change. He begins with a definition: "I would suggest that *a transformed place is that kind of city that pursues fundamental changes, a stable future and the sustaining and enhancing of all of life rooted in a vision bigger than mere urban politics.*"[13] And then he lists twelve key indicators of a transformed city. We don't share them as an exhaustive list, but as an example of one pastor's attempt to change the scoreboard. Similar to the Social Change Model we looked at earlier, Smith looks at altering a city as a series of concentric circles. He starts with the church, although we suspect he'd agree that there's an individual level necessary before that.

Nonetheless, his four concentric circles are church, community, society and creation. In each area he has listed a number of measurable goals his church and other churches of downtown Montreal are committed to. Those goals are as follows:

LOCAL CHURCH LEVEL

- An increasing number of churches actively involved in the spiritual transformation of their city
- The people of God animated by a passionate spirituality involved in concrete acts of reconciliation and justice for the welfare of the city

COMMUNITY OR NEIGHBORHOOD LEVEL

- Leaders desirous to see the people of God use their gifts (in partnership with other churches) to demonstrate the good news in all aspects of the city
- Equality (equity) in economics, social policy, infrastructure, housing, public transportation and education
- Happy and well-developed children and youth, living in peace with God, themselves and others, guided by good spiritual values that enrich their lives and allow them to reach their full potential and the welfare of the city
- A decline in the rate of suicide
- Healthy adults, great marriages, vibrant families (including decreasing rates of AIDS, STDs)

SOCIETY OR CITYWIDE LEVEL

- Multiple institutional opportunities for the most vulnerable to reconnect joyfully with a city that cares for all its populations
- A decline in violence in the city
- A decline of sexual and physical abuse against women and children

CREATION LEVEL

- Beautiful cities and regions as artistic expressions and the heritage of the community are more deeply valued
- A reduction of pollution for a better and more wholesome environment[14]

We like these as a broad set of goals for the church to have. Rather than aiming at domination, they set our hearts toward bringing regeneration, beauty and life to our neighborhoods, the very work God's midwives are meant to attend to. They hold the space. They offer a different narrative. They are a far cry from many churches' goals, which often revolve around expanding buildings, paying down debt and increasing numbers.

An example of this style of mission can be found in Tampa, Florida. There you'll find an amazing church (or collective of microchurches) called Underground. It was started in the summer of 2006 by about fifty Christians from traditional churches who decided to form seven house-based church groups. Led by Brian Sanders, it has grown to a dynamic movement of missional communities that have at heart a desire to engage every kind of evil in their city with prayerful action. Membership at Underground requires that you either launch a new missional initiative or join an existing one. In other words, literally everyone at Underground has embraced a commitment to sacrificial missional service. They are infiltrating every level of Tampa society, with a number of campus groups in local elementary, middle and high schools, as well as nearby universities and a community college. Beyond that, members of Underground have launched microchurches in homes, pubs and community centers, each seeking to address different issues, such as human trafficking, a lack of self-esteem in young people, prostitution, loneliness among the aged, absentee fathering, domestic violence, racial discrimination, mental health issues, homelessness and hunger. There are doula services, a juvenile corrections ministry, an improv theater company, a ministry for single mothers, a "beer and Bible" gathering in an Ybor City pub and more, indicating how broadly they've proliferated their missional responses to their city.

This is a church focused entirely on engaging Tampa at the individual, interpersonal, community, institutional and structural levels, seeking to bring about social change that sets people free, ends suffering and points people to Jesus. They are midwifing the world God is giving birth to.

THE TINY MAN ON THE GIGANTIC PLINTH

If you've ever visited Trafalgar Square in central London you'll know it is dominated by Nelson's Column, which is flanked by two fountains and guarded by four monumental lions. Horatio Nelson, the vice admiral who commanded the British fleet at the Battle of Trafalgar, surveys the city from 185 feet in the air. The square features four plinths that display the statues of once-famous Britons. Well, at least three of them do. After installing likenesses of George IV and Generals Napier and Havelock on three of the plinths, the Fourth Plinth remained unadorned from the mid-1800s.

That is, until 1999 when the first of a series of temporary artworks was placed on it. Created by the English artist Mark Wallinger, it was called *Ecce Homo* (Behold the Man) and depicted Jesus simply as he was presented to the baying crowd by Pontius Pilate in John 19. A life-size sculpture of a near-naked man, covered only by a loin cloth, his hands secured behind his back, his head shaved and crowned by thorns, the statue of Jesus is dwarfed by the enormous plinth upon which it stood. By comparison, the super-sized generals Napier and Havelock are like giants, and the statue of King George has him resplendent astride a mighty horse. Surrounded by enormous and opulent symbols of the power and majesty of imperial Britain, Wallinger's statue of the tiny, frail, unadorned Jesus is breathtaking in its simplicity. Jonathan Hill described the sculpture this way: "This Jesus rejected the trappings of power exemplified in his surroundings and appeared weak and helpless. But the presence of such weakness here, at the heart of power, was itself a kind of strength. It seemed a powerful and moving representation of the topsy-turvy values that Jesus himself preached.["15]

Figure 7.3. Mark Wallinger's statue *Ecce Homo* in Trafalgar Square

We share this image of the tiny Christ on the gigantic plinth because we think it is a profound metaphor for the role the church needs to adopt in society today. The church shouldn't withdraw from the town square. We want it to be part of the cultural, economic, political and social landscapes of our city. The church should desire to contribute in a way that alters the direction of human history to the glory of God. But we know, because of the checkered history of our involvement in culture in the past, that we must adopt a more judicious stance toward the system. Wallinger's statue gives us a picture of our challenge today. The church wants to ascend the plinth, to be visible in the town square, but the church should also want to subvert the system, to appear as a counterpoint to the love of money, military and muscle that appears to obsess our culture.

This is why we think the metaphor of the midwife and this illustration of Mark Wallinger's *Ecce Homo* are so helpful. They are alternatives to the agenda of "Christian dominionism," the impulse of conservative Christians to seek political and cultural power. We want the church to be in attendance at the birthing of God's kingdom, but we are not advocating that the church have dominion over society. The term *dominionism* is generally used to describe the belief by some that the Bible teaches Christians should take control of all earthly institutions and steer society toward the values of the church; that is, toward a kind of theocratic Christendom. Dominionism tends to come in two flavors: Christian Reconstructionism, the belief that the laws of Scripture should supersede secular law; and the New Apostolic Reformation, which teaches that Christians should take the peaks of the so-called seven mountains of culture: government, religion, media, family, business, education, and arts and entertainment. We hope we've pointed out that it is God and God alone who births the kingdom. We are merely God's attendants. But we've also tried to point out the kingdom is more like a mustard shrub than a cedar tree. The church should rightly desire influence. But not control.

Malcolm Gladwell explores this idea in his book *David and Goliath: Underdogs, Misfits, and the Art of Battling Giants*, in which he addresses how the small, underresourced revolutionary can overcome apparently insurmountable odds. Gladwell has long been preoccupied with how people alter their worlds. He is fascinated by the topic of innovation, and seems continually to be trying to answer the question about how people innovate in such a way as to change things for everyone. In *David and Goliath* he appears to conclude that *adversity* is the key. He begins the book by retelling the Old Testament story of the battle-hardened giant killed by the slingshot of the shepherd David, a boy who had never seen war. What David had seen, though, was his flock terrorized by wild animals, and he had acquired a sling and the skill to use it. The lessons absorbed elsewhere transferred that day, his confidence in his abilities was high, and the giant fell. Many people there had slings, but only one had the personality to take on a giant. Gladwell concludes the Davids of this world who defeat the Goliaths of convention and tradition are usually those capable of persevering through rejection, repudiation and setbacks in order to make the world work differently.

Of course, we would say that God gave David the victory that day, and that it wasn't just won on the strength of his personality. Indeed, it seems throughout Scripture that God chooses the unlikely or the weak—the small people—to reveal his greatness, so that no one believes it was ever entirely up to human agency.

Gladwell quotes George Bernard Shaw, who said, "The reasonable man adapts himself to the world; the unreasonable one persists in trying to adapt the world to himself. Therefore all progress depends on the unreasonable man."[16] He then points out that such "unreasonable" people usually emerge toughened by hardship, acquainted with suffering, intolerant of the status quo and possessing certain skills fired in the kiln of adversity. These are the people who most often prevail. These are the ones through whom God seems most inclined to work. They are the tiny people who ascend the gigantic plinth and help us all to see things differently. They are the slight deviation from expectation, they occupy that space between the bizarre and the boring, and they are our giant-killers.

CHANGING THE WORLD THROUGH OUR WORK

8

From a pound of iron, that costs little,
a thousand watch-springs can be made,
whose value becomes prodigious. The pound
you have received from the Lord—use it faithfully.

ROBERT SCHUMANN

ecently, there was five minutes of furor on social media over a noted pastor's tweet about the role of preaching in a Christian's life: "The most important moment each week in the life of the Christian is the preaching event in the local church."[1]

Tweeted like a real preacher, you might say. Aside from ascribing most-important status to the very contribution he makes to the life of his church, and the assumption that learning from God's Word is an "event," the tweet betrayed the chasm between the Christian's Sunday experience and their lives throughout the rest of the week. For the record, we think gathering around the Bible and collectively struggling with its implications for our daily lives is an essential practice for all churches. However, to assign central importance to a function of the church that only one person can do each week (preaching, as it's understood in most churches) is concerning, to say the least. But more than that, it minimizes the contributions that most Christians can make to serving God in and through their vocations. If the church is serious about midwifing the birth of the new creation in every level of society, by embracing collaboration with neighbors and other like-minded groups and by finding common purpose for the common good, we cannot ignore the fact that churches are full of people who are practicing these skills every day in their places of work.

"DECLERICALIZING" THE CHURCH

The midwifing work of the church occurs when the followers of Christ enter fully into the very fabric of the society in which they find themselves. Preachers will certainly make a contribution, but so will schoolteachers, realtors, lawyers, farmers, nurses, etc. In fact, significant cultural change only occurs when so-called lay-people are equipped and inspired to reflect on their vocations through the lens of the gospel. It seems that this is our only hope for broadening the church's current two-pronged strategy for engaging culture: fighting a culture war, or retreating to the margins of society. British missiologist Lesslie Newbigin was all for the church making public pronouncements on issues of the day, but he said these statements needed to be lived out by Christians grappling with solutions in their public life. Real culture change occurs when the church sees the mission of God take root in the marketplace. He wrote,

> This priesthood has to be exercised in the life of the world. It is in the ordinary secular business of the world that the sacrifices of love and obedience are to be offered to God. It is in

the context of secular affairs that the mighty power released into the world through the work of Christ is to be manifested. The Church gathers every Sunday, the day of resurrection and of Pentecost, to renew its participation in Christ's priesthood. But the exercise of this priesthood is not within the walls of the Church but in the daily business of the world.[2]

As a result, Newbigin called for a "declericalizing" of the church and an equal rediscovery of the importance of lay leaders who help congregations "to share with one another the actual experience of their weekday work and to seek illumination from the gospel for their daily secular duty."[3] That phrase was important to Newbigin. He believed that all of culture—the arts, business, health, education, politics—could be shaped by the values of God's kingdom if ordinary Christians working in all those fields could be equipped to think Christianly about the nature of their work. And he believed that clergy were limited in their ability to shape their congregations in this way.

According to Newbigin, the church needed to develop professional coaches (our term, not his) that sat under biblical authority and the teaching of ministers and bridged the gap between the rarefied world of the clergy and the everyday world of the parishioner. When one church leader pushed back against this by accusing Newbigin of trying to eliminate the clergy, the old missionary retorted wisely, "I'm not trying to eliminate the clergy. I'm trying to eliminate the *laity*." It's a clever line. In effect, he wanted to ordain all believers to the work to which God has called them. He wrote,

> The kingship of God, present in Jesus, concerns the whole of human life in its public as well as its private aspects. There is no basis in scripture for the withdrawal of the public aspect of human life from that obedience which the disciple owes to

the Lord. The question, therefore, is not: "What grounds can be shown for Christian involvement in public life?" It is: "What grounds can be shown for the proposal to withdraw from the rule of Christ the public aspects of our human living?" The answer is: "None."[4]

Having said that, Newbigin was no fan of anticlericalism, either. After all, he wanted to ordain *everyone*. It's just that he saw the role of clerics as being to serve, nourish, sustain and guide the priestly mission work of all believers, in the same ways Paul called leaders "to equip the saints for the work of ministry" (Eph 4:12). In this respect, to return to the pastor's tweet we began with, the "preaching event" would be far more important than even he realizes if its function is to do all that. And yet, most Christians report that the preaching they hear each week rarely addresses the practicalities of how to perform our vocations as kingdom people and how to seek illumination from the gospel for it. Amy Sherman, in her book on vocational stewardship, *Kingdom Calling*, points out,

> More often, though, [Christian professionals] are simply instructed to be people of strong integrity and to seek to win coworkers for Christ. These emphases on ethics and evangelism are needed and valuable, but they are insufficient for equipping Christians to steward their vocational power to advance foretastes of the kingdom. We need to get beyond the status quo.[5]

Sherman says that most discussions about the integration of faith and work/vocation are oriented around those two primary concerns—ethics and evangelism—with some lesser consideration given to enrichment and experience. When it comes to what kind of support or training workers receive in their churches it's usually in ethics or evangelism. It's rarely in enrichment or experience.

First and foremost, Sherman explains, Christians are strongly encouraged to think about how they can be personally ethical at work—that is, how not to scrimp, cut corners or be deceitful in the conduct of their business. Second, there's a slightly lesser emphasis on Christian workers being encouraged to evangelize their colleagues or host a lunchtime Bible study or such. Third, there's even less emphasis on a Christian perspective on how our work enriches us personally and contributes to our sense of well-being. And fourth, there's hardly any emphasis on our actual experience of our work and how that work has any intrinsic or extrinsic meaning and purpose.

But more than that, says Sherman, usually all four areas are discussed in highly individualistic terms. When clergy teach about ethics at work, it's nearly always in terms of personal morality and never about how to lead your organization into a greater sense of corporate ethics. Evangelism is taught in terms of one-on-one personal witness, but not how to reflect on your work in light of the gospel. We think about how our work might enrich us personally and how it could foster an individual sense of purpose and meaning, but we don't think of it contributing to the greater sense of good. Sherman draws on James Hunter's work to ask whether the largely missing piece in discussions about Christians and their work has been a vision for institutional transformation for the greater good of society through a demonstration of the Christian values of justice and shalom. She quotes Hunter as saying that Christians must "challenge all structures that dishonor God, dehumanize people, and neglect or do harm to the creation."[6] If the church is to midwife the birth of the new creation then this has to have implications for how Christians view their work. It is summarized by this table:

Table 8.1. Aspects of work for Christians

Aspect	Individual Lens	Societal Lens
Ethics	Be personally moral at work.	Explore ways your organization can be more ethically responsible.
Evangelism	Share the gospel with your colleagues.	Allow the values of the gospel to affect the whole culture of your workplace.
Enrichment	Make sure your work maximizes your potential.	Make sure your organization maximizes the well-being of the broader society.
Experience	Consider how your work enhances your sense of purpose.	Reform the practice of your industry to align with the values of justice and shalom.

THE PLACE GOD CALLS YOU TO

No doubt you've come across Frederick Buechner's maxim, "The place God calls you to is the place where your deep gladness and the world's deep hunger meet." As far as it goes, it's a good rule of thumb for thinking about your vocation. But it doesn't really go very far.

Christians do (or should) want to meet the world's great needs. And they want to be glad about the contribution they can make. But there are other factors in play. For example, will anyone pay you to do that work? And are you any good at it? Amy Sherman writes about finding the sweet spot in the nexus between My Passions and Gifts (your deep gladness), The World's Needs (or deep hunger) and a third consideration, God's Priorities.[7] But the vast majority of people are beholden to the forces of the labor market. If no one pays me to satisfy my passions, the world's needs and God's priorities, I'll starve. So there needs to be another consideration we'd like to add: Your Paycheck. Another way to look at it is this:

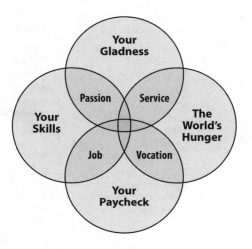

Figure 8.1. The place God calls you to

In this diagram, the nexus Buechner talks about between your deep gladness and the world's deep hunger could be characterized as your sphere of service. For example, the world needs unwanted kids to be taken care of, and fostering kids brings you a great sense of personal enrichment. But when it comes to our employment, many Christians find themselves in the nexus between their skills and their paycheck. That's called a job in this diagram. Likewise, many Christians' passion (the nexus between their skills and their gladness) is also separate from their job or their vocation. The church needs to be realistic about this. Aiming for the sweetest spot of all—the nexus between our gladness, the world's needs, our skills and getting paid for it—is the goal. And if we read James Hunter's *To Change the World* accurately, he's saying that those Christians who find themselves in that spot are capable of very great good and very great influence in society. But the church can't be insensitive to the fact that many Christians don't get to that sweet spot. We need to be equipping people to live out the values of the kingdom of God, whether that's in their job, their service, their vocation or their passion, or the combination of some or all of them.

How are we to find that place to which God calls us, and how are we to contribute to changing culture through our employed work? We'd like to suggest a few ways:

1. Foster an eschatology that sustains our work. Maintaining fidelity with the values of the kingdom of God in our work takes courage and perseverance. Lesslie Newbigin pointed out that our political and religious activity alone won't birth the reign of God. We can be a sign and foretaste, but the unfurling of the kingdom is God's work. There is something both wonderfully freeing and terrifyingly onerous about that. We are commissioned as God's servants, while freed from the ultimate responsibility of giving birth to God's reign. What will sustain us in the work of influencing and shaping culture through our vocations? We suggest the church needs a better eschatology.

When it comes to theological discussions, eschatology often gets put in the corner or the too-hard basket. Many of you might have grown up in Christian homes where discussions and sermons about the "end times" were either highly contentious or downright frightening. Those who survived second coming conventions (with their timelines and marks of the beast) often managed to keep their faith intact by quarantining eschatology away from the center of their theology. They would make vague statements like, "Well, I know Jesus is coming back, and that's all I need to know." We've heard a few eschatology-shy Christians use that cute line, "Jesus is coming back and I want to be on the welcoming committee, not the planning committee." But that's really just a way of avoiding thinking about an area of the Bible that was for too long a battleground, not a source of comfort. The fact is, though, that Paul refers to Christians as those who have set their hope on Christ (2 Cor 1:10). As the hope-filled ones, surely *all* theology is eschatological. Eschatology is not a self-contained unit of study that can be hived off easily from the rest of Scripture. As theologian Johannes Baptist Metz says, "Eschatology is not a discipline beside other disciplines, but that basic discipline which determines, forms, and shapes every theological statement, especially those concerning the world."[8]

Hope is central for sustaining Christians, because Christianity is a thoroughly future-oriented worldview. Christians hope not only for their own future destiny, but we hold hope also for the future of the world. But we don't feel ultimately responsible for it. That's the beauty of biblical eschatology. It invites us to live in the dialectic between freedom and responsibility.

Some time ago, I (Michael) met a human rights worker from the Philippines. She was working in the midst of intractable poverty on the streets of Manila, addressing a pervasive culture of corruption and inequity. She saw very few victories in her long, long march toward a just and fair society. I asked her what sustained her in her grinding labors on behalf of the poor and marginalized, suggesting that perhaps those tiny victories were encouraging enough to keep her going. Not at all, she declared strongly. What kept her going, she explained, was knowing that it *wasn't* her work to bring the kingdom of God to Manila. That was God's work. Her eschatological perspective both freed her from crushing responsibility as well as galvanizing her resolve to continue. David Bosch explains how eschatology (or Paul's apocalyptic, as he terms it) does this:

> Paul's apocalyptic is not an invitation to ethical passivity, but to active participation in God's redemptive will. He is charged with enlarging in this world the domain of God's coming world. . . . His involvement is in what is at hand rather than in what will be. Authentic apocalyptic hope thus compels ethical seriousness. It is impossible to believe in God's coming triumph without being agitators for God's kingdom

here and now, and without an ethic that strains and labors to move God's creation toward the realization of God's promise in Christ.[9]

A proper biblical eschatology shouldn't propel us toward wanting to escape from the world. As we noted earlier, Lesslie Newbigin said the gospel doesn't offer a way of escape for the redeemed soul out of history, but calls us to join the work of God to bring history to its true end. Or as Metz puts it, Christian hope is not flight *from* the world, but flight *with* the world (into the future). Metz is not calling for a form of solidarity with the world that passively accepts whatever it says or desires. He definitely calls on Christians to renounce the world, or to resist being conformed to this world, but, as he explains, "The Christian is moved to flee and to renounce the world not because he despises the world but because he hopes in the future of the world as proclaimed in God's promises . . . A faith which is guided by such a hope is primarily not a doctrine, but an initiative for the passionate innovating and changing of the world toward the Kingdom of God."[10]

In other words, a belief in the coming kingdom of God doesn't evoke passivity. It mobilizes the believer to embrace our common mission to be a sign, foretaste and instrument of the coming reign of God. Every Christian is called to embody in their life and work what it means to live within the reign of God. Seeing our work as our mission isn't just about using our place of business as an arena for personal witnessing. It involves recognizing that we can, in part, fulfill our calling to serve God through the very work that we do. We are called to resist being conformed to the values of this world, not by withdrawal from it, but by entering it with gusto and bringing glimpses of the world-to-come to all. Newbigin wrote, "We do indeed look forward with eager longing to that Christian society which is the final goal of all God's creative and redemptive love, but until that day we are called upon to seek on earth a society which, as far as may be granted to us, reflects the glory of the city to which we look forward."[11]

Workers need the support and encouragement to consider how their role as a teacher, parent, lawyer, artist, businessperson, etc., reflects the glory of that future city. They need an eschatological vision that shapes their values and frames their daily work in terms of their future hope. We can't say it better than N. T. Wright does in *Surprised by Hope*:

> The point of the resurrection . . . is that *the present bodily life is not valueless just because it will die*. . . . What you do with your body in the present matters because God has a great future in store for it. . . . What you *do* in the present—by painting, preaching, singing, sewing, praying, teaching, building hospitals, digging wells, campaigning for justice, writing poems, caring for the needy, loving your neighbor as yourself—*will last into God's future*. These activities are not simply ways of making the present life a little less beastly, a little more bearable, until the day when we leave it behind altogether (as the hymn so mistakenly puts it . . .). They are part of what we may call *building for God's kingdom*.[12]

This realization doesn't come easily. Working out the ethics of the kingdom in our place of work is not all smooth sailing. In fact, it shouldn't be! Plotting goodness and justice in our vocational pursuits in the world can be met with opposition, possibly even to the point where we must face decisions that could cost us our jobs. The deeper our convictions, the more likely we are to make vocational choices that require an unwavering trust in God's lead, rather than our own ability or skill.

After many years of grappling with vocational questions and seeking to live out his faith values within the company he worked for, Andy Balch of Glendale, California, decided it was time to begin a new venture. He changed jobs and started to work for a friend's startup business, hiring and training employees from underprivileged families who otherwise may be overlooked or taken advantage of. He wrote to us about his work:

> Living out my faith in my work begins with the simple things like honoring the guys that are working for me, even in small, seemingly insignificant ways. The way I speak to them, the way I listen and my refusal to settle for mediocre work when I know these guys are capable of more. In this line of work, it is so easy to view these employees as a product or an expendable tool, but truthfully, they are hard-working people who want to be respected and honored just like I do. I'm honest and up front with the guys, paying them a fair wage, getting them the training they need not only to succeed in their day to day work which benefits the company but also to move them forward in their careers. I'll often ask the guys about their goals and how I can help him move toward their life aspirations. In this industry, my way of doing business often costs more money than I'd like. I could get more work done by paying less and hiring more guys. But that's not what God has called me to do and I'm deeply content with this alternative way.[13]

2. Ordain people to their job/service/vocation/passion. Perhaps you've attended an ordination service or have been ordained yourself. The ordination ceremony usually begins with the candidate being asked to affirm several doctrinal statements, after which the person officiating asks, "Will you now take your ordained place among the people of God, as an agent and sign of the good news of Jesus Christ, serving them and not lording it over them, leading them in humility, compassion and patience?" Once the candidate confirms this statement she or he is then asked to make promises about proclaiming the Bible, celebrating the sacraments, faithfully caring for God's people, etc. After that, the congregation is invited to declare that they will continually pray for the candidate and uphold and encourage him or her in ministry, or words to that effect.

I (Michael) am regularly invited to speak at the ordination services of my former students, and I find them to be beautifully moving occasions. It's not common to observe a person laid bare before an assembly of peers, pledging his or her life to a higher cause, promising to selflessly serve and love others. In fact, there's something spine tingling about a formal ceremony of love, devotion and commitment. It happens at weddings and inductions into the armed forces. Such ceremonies don't happen every week. But why not? If the church is to call its members to be midwives at the birth of the new creation, why don't we ordain them to it?

The term *vocation* comes from the Latin *vocare*, meaning "to call." It is the calling in our spirits that gives rise to the employment we choose. Often we only use the term *vocation* to refer to people entering the priesthood or the clergy. We assume that the calling to do so has to have come from God. God calls people into ordained ministry. We routinely refer to people "receiving the call" to Christian service, whether to church leadership or to the mission field. But this is faulty thinking. It comes from an era when it was believed that reality was divided into two separate spheres—the sacred and the profane. This is called dualism, and the Christian movement has struggled with it for virtually its whole existence.

Dualism separates the sacred from the profane, the holy from the unholy, the in from the out. The sacred realm obviously includes God and is supposed to be clearly present in church services, the Mass, Bible studies, theological seminaries, etc. The profane realm is the rest of life—having sex, gardening, going to the art gallery, eating, renovating the house, sports, working out, etc. It's not so much that God is absent from these places, but we just don't presume that God is particularly present in them. We talk routinely about the "world out there." What else can that mean, other than that we the church-people are "in here"! This dualism has over 1,700 years created Christians that cannot relate their interior faith to their exterior practice, and this affects their ethics, their lifestyles and their capacity to see their work as a godly, midwifing activity.

If we presume that God is most keenly present in church, we begin to assume God is like the greatest priest, the most perfect rector, preacher, minister, pastor, vicar, reverend or cleric. If the focus of God the Vicar is on church meetings then it follows that to imitate God, like a child does his or her parent, means that the greatest vocation we can adopt is that of church leadership. We have no difficulty believing that people who enter the priesthood or vocational ministry are doing so because they are following God. But we can't say the same about other people who decide to pursue a legal career, or accountancy, or nursing, or a myriad of other vocations. Why can't they similarly be following God's calling on their lives? And we must note here, the majority of people in these spiritually authoritative positions are men, which, of course, immobilizes the population of women to an even greater degree.

With this in mind, we propose you develop an ordination ceremony for ordaining all believers to the work to which God calls them. It won't necessarily be the work of preaching the Bible or administering the sacraments. But it will be the work of honoring God in all that they do. In this respect, we follow Martin Luther's formulation for the priesthood of all believers: "As far as that goes, we are all consecrated priests through baptism."[14] The only differentiation that Luther saw was between the kind of work that God has given us to do, not in the status of that work. In other words, a priest is no more called to her work than a doctor is to hers. He went on,

There is no true, basic difference between laymen and priests, princes and bishops, between religious and secular, except for the sake of office and work, but not for the sake of status. They are all of the spiritual estate. . . . But they do not all have the same work to do.[15]

In God's scheme of things, each Christian receives a particular calling in this life, the purpose of which is to serve others. Luther continues, "Everyone must benefit and serve every other by means of his own work or office so that in this way many kinds of work may be done for the bodily and spiritual welfare of the community, just as all the members of the body serve one another."[16]

And this is key in Luther's thinking. Our work must be oriented to the service of others. You might have read the faux Luther quote, "The Christian shoemaker does his Christian duty not by putting little crosses on the shoes, but by making good shoes, because God is interested in good craftsmanship." Well, he didn't actually write that. The idea that God is pleased with our work because he likes quality work might ring true in modern America, but it wasn't a notion that Luther seemed persuaded by. Luther's view of our work was shaped by his insistence that it should be completed in service of the neighbor and of the world. As Frederick Gaiser wrote of Luther's view, "God likes shoes (and good ones!) not for their own sake, but because the neighbor needs shoes."[17] Therefore, it is reasonable to ordain a cobbler to the world-serving work of shoemaking.

As far as we can tell Luther didn't claim we should ordain all believers, but it's a logical extension of his thinking. Luther thought there was no biblical basis for the sacramental character of ordination, believing it had been devised by the church entirely to elevate the clergy over the laity. Typically, though, rather than abolishing ordination, he redesigned it from a sacramental role to a teaching one. We think that ordaining teachers in this way is entirely useful. But we'd like to ordain that shoemaker as well.

In my (Christiana's) faith community we have developed an equipping process titled "Life Compass: The Kingdom of God as Our True North." In this process, participants reflect on their life story, their unique wiring, their grounding values and their deep desires. The eight-week process culminates in presentations by each participant sharing a vision statement that pulls all these aspects together in an articulation of their particular contribution in God's kingdom to impact the world. These are not mission statements or career aspirations. These are glimpses and pictures of their preferred future. As visions are shared, the rest of the community affirms and surrounds each person in prayer, blessing and commissioning them forward. These visions are a metaphorical compass for moving toward more of the kingdom of God. They are an everyday grid to guide us in making life decisions, big and small, regularly prompting us to ask the question, Does this decision move me toward my vision or away from it? We view the entirety of this process, in essence, as a sacred ceremony of ordination.

3. Create a new matrix for measuring success. I (Michael) have a friend who interned with a big multinational law firm while he was completing law school. After graduating David earned a much coveted position in the company and looked set for a promising career as a litigator. There were suggestions he could soon be on a track toward becoming a partner in the firm. He got married, bought a nice house, and on appearances was hitting all the markers for a successful life and career. Except, he was working sixty-five to seventy hours a week, spent hardly any time with his new wife and paid people to take care of his nice house and garden. As Christians, David and Jenny decided to stop one day and reflect on just how successful their lives really were. They concluded that while they scored high according to cultural markers of success they were in fact failing to live out the values of the kingdom.

David quit his sought-after position with the city firm and set up his own suburban practice just around the corner from his home. Challenged by the plight of refugees and asylum seekers, he decided to focus on immigration law. Today, David is one of a handful of accredited immigration specialists in his city, working on visa applications, merits reviews and judicial reviews, and has established a reputation for successfully solving difficult immigration cases. He has been a godsend to many asylum seekers over the years. He is regularly consulted by lawyers and migration agents on complex issues of immigration law. He rides a bicycle to work each day. He eats dinner with his wife and children every night.

It's true he doesn't earn as much money as he would have if he'd ended up a partner in the big city firm. But he considers himself more successful at following Christ than he ever could have before. And he is contributing to the common good in ways he could never have imagined before.

In sharing this story we are not implying that it is not possible to mirror the work of God in a big law firm. But we share it because a lot of Christian lawyers don't ever seem to take the time to sit down and ask what constitutes success in their careers. Is success only ever to be assessed based on billable hours, the prestige of your firm, the size of your house and your financial portfolio? Is there a different matrix for measuring success for Christian workers?

A good place to start is reexamining what we do with our time and money. Much has been written on how to steward the money we have, how to invest it for long-term security and how to give it away, so long as it factors into our overall budget. Spending time well is certainly another common topic of stewardship. Yet we're interested in what it looks like to challenge the ways in which our cultural myths and blind spots have deterred us away from the instruction of Jesus on this topic. We think it is much more costly and holistic than simply building a hefty investment plan and working harder at self-care.

Two of our favorite teachers and practitioners in this area are Mark and Lisa Scandrette. In their book *Free: Spending your Time and Money on What Matters Most*, they offer a compelling invitation to embrace the radical way of Jesus in dealing with our resources, to repent and rejoice in the process, to foster simplicity and generosity, to open our lives to love and ultimately to live free and offer freedom to others. The Scandrettes provide methods, habits and processes for learning what it means to offer up our time and money for what matters most for the sake of the common good. While, for the most part, contemporary Christians do desire a life of more holistic stewardship in the way of Jesus, the Scandrettes warn us that unless practical realities and competencies are addressed, these desires will remain inactive. They write,

> Instead of being free to create beauty, nurture relationships and seek the greater good, many of us feel stuck in lives dictated by the need to pay bills or maintain a certain (often consumptive) standard of living. We can't have it all—the prevailing level of consumption, a life of deeper meaning and relationships and global equity and sustainability. To realize these good dreams we must adjust our values and practices and seek creative solutions.[18]

The Scandrettes suggest we steward our lives with gratitude, trust, contentment and generosity, recognizing that every momentary life choice has dynamic impact on those around us and on those across the globe. This kind of stewardship will alter the world as we know it. And Christians should be on the forefront of ushering in this new economy that God envisions.

Currently, global economics and politics are based on the worst aspects of human nature—fear and greed. No wonder, then, that our societies have become riddled with inequality, violence and mistrust. It is therefore vital that the followers of Jesus in every sphere of society seek to build cultures of trust, being prepared to take risks for the common good. And it is imperative that their churches provide the support, nurture and encouragement to continue in this task. What will they be aiming at? We suggest their work could involve things such as:

- Bringing human consumption into balance with the needs of the earth
- Realigning our economic priorities so that all persons have access to an adequate and meaningful means of earning a living for themselves and their families
- Democratizing our institutions to route power to people and communities
- Replacing the dominant culture of materialism with cultures grounded in life-affirming values of cooperation, caring, compassion and community
- Integrating the material and spiritual aspects of humanity so that we become whole persons for the greater good

This list could be much longer. But we hope you take the point. Why aren't more churches working on developing lists of key indicators of a successful God-honoring work life for their members?

4. Expect greater things from industry leaders. All workers can transform their world by the performance of their vocation, but it makes sense that industry leaders can affect greater cultural change than others. This isn't to minimize the contribution to culture made by the hardworking and devoted Christian math teacher. But it does recognize that those educators who develop the math curriculum are going to have wider influence. Earlier, we referred to Ed, the Californian schools administrator. He is helping to shape the education system in Northern California as well as revitalizing the struggling neighborhoods around his schools. It's not unreasonable to recognize that, while every Christian builder can express their faith through ethical business practices, the fair treatment of workers and a commitment to environmental sustainability, certain big developers, architects and town planners are industry leaders that can express faithfulness to their calling and meaningful local presence. In this respect they partner with God, who is shaping the cities we live in. Whether they are businesspeople, leaders in the health and education sector, legislators, litigators or city supervisors, they can help shape the conditions for the birth of the new creation by reflecting on their work through the lens of the gospel. We're not talking about getting creationism into the school science curriculum or reserving land for church buildings in new housing developments. It's about using influence as Christians to open the space for God to birth something new.

Similarly, as we said earlier, the church can't return to the days of trying to impose Christianity on culture in an attempt to make everyone Christian. But the church can tilt culture in a way that makes the Christian lifestyle acceptable, welcome and appealing.

In 2015, Franklin Graham posted this Facebook status: "Can you imagine what a difference it would make if Christians ran for every office at all levels across our country—city council, school board, Mayor? We need to get involved and take a stand for biblical values and morals before it's too late. If you agree share this."[19] Aside from the fact that many Christians can't agree on which political party to support let alone what stand they should take on such "biblical values and morals," it's hard to imagine this kind of concerted political effort doing anything other than alienating most of society.

However, expecting that influential industry leaders can affect culture positively in line with the values of the kingdom is entirely reasonable. It's not a top-down imposition of Christian laws, but a bottom-up infiltration of every sector of society, which is good news for everyone.

As Paul says to Timothy, those with wealth and influence have certain responsibilities expected of them:

> Command those who are rich in this present world not to be arrogant nor to put their hope in wealth, which is so uncertain, but to put their hope in God, who richly provides us with everything for our enjoyment. Command them to do good, to be rich in good deeds, and to be generous and willing to share. In this way they will lay up treasure for themselves as a firm foundation for the coming age, so that they may take hold of the life that is truly life. (1 Tim 6:17-19 NIV)

If you've ever played Monopoly you've probably bought or sold Reading Railroad. The now-defunct railroad is named after the Pennsylvania city of Reading, through which coal trucks used to rumble on their way to the port of Philadelphia. Sadly, today Reading has fallen on hard times. It is one of the most crime-ridden, poverty-stricken cities in the United States.

Into this broken city came Craig Poole, a hotel manager with fifty years of experience in revitalizing distressed areas and hotels. At a time in his life when he felt the pull to make an even greater kingdom impact through is work, Craig came upon ReWire, a ministry that equips Christians to view their vocation through the lens of missional spirituality.[20] Coached by a ReWire staff member, Poole left a successful job in Pittsburgh to move to Reading to run the Doubletree Hotel on Seventh and Penn Streets precisely because the city was broken. As a Christian businessman he sees it as his role to help make a difference for communities that have been forgotten. Indeed, he didn't just want to run a profitable hotel. He also wanted to change a city.

Poole's overriding question when taking over the Doubletree was, How do you use your business model for the good of the community? He started by simply employing the poor, in particular helping former prison inmates get a second chance. In no time he had ten ex-offenders on the payroll and many more wanting jobs. So he helped found the local county Criminal Justice Employment Council, dedicated to finding jobs for former inmates reentering society. His impact on the city was becoming obvious, so the council invited him to join the Main Street Board, where he has helped to revitalize local businesses, oversee renovations to decaying buildings, launch a flea market and even help establish a microbrewery.

And soon one thing led to another. He began a partnership with several school districts and community organizations to help special-needs students find jobs and vocational training. He was also honored as the Latino Business Partner of the Year.

Poole tells the story of how he once invited teenage gang members to join him for dinner in the Doubletree's fine dining restaurant. He bought them all steak and shrimp dinners. Some of them had never used a cloth napkin before. He explains, "Great food is not just meant for the rich. It is also meant for the poor, broken and lost because it nourishes their souls, bodies and minds."[21]

We don't all own hotels, but we can honor others and practice generosity and hospitality, like Poole does. Craig Poole says he just wants to do God's will. And God is leading him outside the doors of his hotel lobby into the grim streets of Reading to bring glimpses of a new world being born.

CHANGING THE WORLD THROUGH PLACECRAFTING

9

What I stand for is what I stand on.

WENDELL BERRY

W henever you think about altering the world for the better in alignment with the values of the reign of God, you can't help but imagine what the future could be like if we were achieving our hope. What, for example, would our cities and towns look like if we were fully available as the instruments for doing God's will in those places? We googled images for "cities of the future," and you can see what came up first in our search (figure 9.1).[1]

Try it for yourself. All the images that appeared in our search were just variations on the one above—pristine, high-rise, metal-and-glass visions of the future of our cities. At least it's not the Los Angeles of 2019 as depicted in *Blade Runner*. It seems we've moved on from the dystopian images of dark, bleak, wet, overcrowded cities that many futuristic films portray. But are the new visions much better?

Figure 9.1. Imagined city of the future

The metallic cities currently being built by developers and town planners might look appealing, but are they fostering the kinds of neighborhoods we need? We think it is important for churches to contribute to shaping cities, towns and suburbs as part of their culture-altering agenda precisely because the built environment helps shape the quality of human community. We all know about the manicured lawns and neat houses of suburbs where nobody knows their neighbors' names. These neighborhoods look peaceful but they hide terrible levels of loneliness, dislocation and, in some cases, violence. These suburbs were designed by developers who were interested chiefly in profit, not community. But as Christians surely we would see our role in shaping culture to include shaping the opportunities for neighborliness and conviviality. N. T. Wright addresses this in his discussion of the mission of the church:

> Thus the church . . . [should] go straight from worshipping in the sanctuary to debating in the council chamber—discussing matters of town planning, of harmonizing and humanizing

beauty in architecture, in green spaces, in road traffic schemes and . . . in environmental work, creative and healthy farming methods, and proper use of resources. If it is true, as I have argued, that the whole world is now God's holy land, we must not rest as long as that land is spoiled and defaced. This is not an extra to the church's mission. It is central.[2]

If the whole world is God's holy land, what kind of cities would God desire? We would answer that God desires the kinds of cities that foster and encourage the values of God's reign—justice, reconciliation, beauty, wholeness, etc. So surely, culture-shaping Christians should be actively engaged in the kind of work Wright describes.

An instructive case study to look at would be the nation-city of Singapore. It has state-of-the-art infrastructure, award-winning architecture and a safe, clean, green environment, with its notoriously enforced public littering laws. It looks immaculate to any tourist or business traveler. But all those clean lines and manicured lawns come at a cost. During the last fifty years, Singapore has experienced an astonishing rate of urbanization that has transformed the tiny island-state into a fast-paced "Asian Tiger." Prior to the aggressive urban planning policies of the twentieth century, Singaporeans—a mix of Chinese, Malay and Indians—lived in kampungs, typical traditional Asian villages. Here, families lived intergenerationally in a mix of poor and middle-class communities. But after independence in the 1960s, demolition teams started carving a swathe through the kampungs, building high-rise glass and chrome monoliths. Villagers were split up and moved into apartments, ranked A, B, C and D housing, depending on each family's financial status. People went from the kampungs, where they knew everybody from grandparents to newborn babies, into skyscrapers where they knew no one. The high-rise boom continues unhindered to this day, as one-hundred-year-old bungalows and once-sprawling, breezy oceanfront gardens are bulldozed to make way for more high-rise housing, commercial properties and shopping malls.

Old Singaporeans can be quite nostalgic about life in the kampungs. They remember them as places with a genuine sense of neighborhood and deep social connection. But many of them were not much more than slums. The social and economic revolution of Lee Kuan Yew delivered remarkable benefits for the people of Singapore in terms of sanitation, education and wealth, but it overlooked the importance of *place* in developing healthy societies. Today, the local press and social commentators bemoan the "ugly Singaporean," who pushes people out of the way to get a seat on a train, complains aggressively when things don't go their way and ignores those in need as though they don't exist. There have been recent city-wide campaigns to stop the ill treatment of domestic workers and the elderly. Some businesses are offering "complain training" to help people cope with the prevalence of belligerent grousing by Singaporeans over the most mundane things. Seah Chiang Nee writes, "Have affluent, educated Singaporeans become too self-centred and insensitive to other people's plights? Can Singapore be considered a First World city with such boorishness? A mature, developed country isn't defined only by wealth and education; it is also about humanity and concern for others."[3]

While it might look magnificent to the visitor, Singaporean society is showing the strain that emerges when people live in such isolated conditions, away from real community. As well as housing, the kampungs provided public space for meaningful social interaction. In the new Singapore, housing is available, but at the cost of public space—those zones where people interact across cultural and socioeconomic lines. A United Nations paper on public space concluded,

Public space generates equality. Where public space is inadequate, poorly designed, or privatized, the city becomes increasingly segregated. Lines are drawn based on religion, ethnicity, gender and economic status because people don't meet or get to know each other. The result can be a polarized city where social tensions are likely to flare up and where social mobility and economic opportunity are stifled.[4]

As we mentioned earlier, similar dynamics are present in suburban or rural contexts in America. Suburban neighborhoods can also reinforce isolation, segregation and exclusion by setting up gated communities and tract homes with high fences and forward-facing (closed) garage doors. Or in rural areas people are separated by acres of land and locked gates and neighbors are forced to commute long distances for the majority of their social interaction. These obstacles are certainly penetrable when seeking to build relationships, but we bring them up here to communicate that our environment can perpetuate human separation in varied contexts, not just urban centers. Our built environments impact our ability to build true community.

Of course, no one is suggesting that Singapore return to the kampungs, but perhaps they need to give greater consideration to the idea of placemaking, or *placecrafting*, as Jennifer Krouse from the Congress for the New Urbanism terms it. Placecrafting is a collaborative process of shaping a community's public areas with a view to maximizing social amenity. While Singapore might look like a city of the future, it has much to teach us about the necessity of paying particular attention to the physical, cultural and social identities that define a place. As Ethan Kent from the Project for Public Spaces explains,

> The current vision of "the future of cities" is void of people, difference, chaos, street life, and interaction—the very qualities

that make cities valuable and viable. While depicting the easily misdirected urban goals of mobility, icon, and open space, these images of the future ignore the qualities that great cities can produce: access, sociability, use, comfort, and identity—the ingredients of place.[5]

Recent studies have shown that the provision of public spaces in cities has considerable social benefits. It can increase economic vitality, reduce public expenditure on health care and urban management, and increase business confidence. But more than that, good public spaces lead to an improved quality of life for residents. They increase a perceived sense of security and safety and promote equality and stability. They also generate cultural vitality and civic pride. And, naturally, they're good for the environment. If churches are serious about changing their context, placecrafting needs to be at the center of their thinking.

PLACECRAFTING AS HOLDING SPACE

Whose role is it to be at the forefront of placecrafting in a neighborhood? We live in a world dominated by the neoliberal capitalist paradigm, with its commitment to profit maximization and cost minimization. The example of Singapore shows what kind of city results from only measuring success in terms of economic prosperity. As a result, property developers and city hall aren't always inclined to take the lead on ensuring that public places are shaped for the development of community. Surely, then, this is a role for people whose worldview is hinged on the transforming power of real relationships. Surely, this is a role for the church. Could the church help influence those Christians who work as town planners, developers and city supervisors, as well as those who are residents or business owners, to build better cities? We see this as an opportunity to make a meaningful contribution in society.

Earlier we identified the key work of a midwife as that of holding the space—choreographing the elements of an environment to facilitate birth. This is similar to the work of a gardener or a farmer. Gardeners technically don't grow anything. The earth does. Gardeners and farmers manipulate or arrange the environment—working with the seasons, tilling the soil, adding water, compost and fertilizer—to aid germination and growth. Placecrafting is a form of gardening. It is concerned with contributing to the shape of our environments in order to allow God's new creation to germinate and flourish.

Christians have a history of shaping the built environments of their cities. In his book *The Spiritual City*, Philip Sheldrake points out the role Christian religious orders had in shaping urban form in medieval cities:

> Later in the Middle Ages, the development of the great Italian city piazzas owed much to the new religious orders, such as the Franciscans, Dominicans, and Servites and their preaching churches. These buildings opened onto large open spaces that enabled crowds to listen to sermons (for example, in Florence the famous piazzas outside the churches of Santa Croce, San Marco, Santa Maria Novella, and Santissima Annunziata). Just as the colonnades of ancient Rome gave birth to the design of the monastic cloister, so in the new laicized city spirituality of the later Middle Ages, the monastic cloister in turn moved out into the city to give birth to the colonnaded piazza. This space offered a vision of the city, metaphorically (because it engendered a concept of public space for intermingling) and also practically (because it opened up new urban vistas).[6]

While it is certainly true that the piazzas of Florence were established during the height of Christendom, and the church no longer has the access or opportunity to influence the built environment of its city today, this doesn't mean the church should retreat from its role in shaping place. Indeed, we don't need to go back as far as the Greek agora or the Roman forum or medieval Florence to see this in action. New England village greens and Midwestern town squares are more recent examples of the link between church and urban form. Today, some churches are doing their best to contribute to placecrafting, and one of the terms they're using is that of the *commons*. Commons were traditionally defined as elements of the environment, such as forests, rivers, fisheries or grazing land that could be shared and used by all. Today, the phrase *urban commons* is used to denote all those public elements that help a healthy society function—public spaces, squares, schools, markets, medical facilities, and other infrastructure. One suburban church has taken seriously their mandate to help fashion commons in their neighborhood.

The 2|42 Community Church in Brighton, Michigan, recently bought an abandoned tennis and racquetball center in town, but instead of refurbishing it as a worship space and using it only for Sunday services, they tried something different. Their minister, David Dummitt, describes the building:

> When I first walked through the abandoned facility, it had been empty for 15 years and was in an extreme state of disrepair. It looked like a location from *The Walking Dead*. There were still shoes on the floor, shorts and towels in the lockers and several tennis balls littering the courts in the expansive building. With stained walls and falling ceiling tiles from extensive water leaks, this place left me uncharacteristically unsure of its potential for redemption.[7]

So he put a sign out front that said, "Coming Soon—You Decide," with a phone number. In effect, 2|42 Community Church handed their building over to their neighbors. Today, it serves as a community center, hosting the School for the Arts and the Commons Café.

"If we followed a normal plan we would have built on the outskirts of our area where land is cheaper and waited for the community to come to us," Dummitt says. "Instead we bought the ugliest place in town—but a place that's close to the people we want to reach."[8]

In the mountain town of Julian, California, two families, the Elisaras and the Parkers, chose to buy a house together and open it as a home of hospitality, hosting town events, trainings and retreats. They call it the Julian Project, seeking not only to use their land and property for the common good but also to be present and participating in their wider context, influencing city decisions, serving on boards, establishing conservation centers, working as rangers, volunteering at the Julian schools and advocating for healthier food, better care of the environment and more intentional town planning that benefits Julian residents at large. For a town whose economy is driven by tourism and agriculture, particularly apple orchards, these two families have been placecrafting for over twenty years, building community and initiating lasting change.

HOW DO YOU CRAFT A PLACE?

Earlier we quoted our great friends Paul Sparks, Tim Soerens and Dwight Friesen from their book *The New Parish*. Their approach to the challenge of placecrafting is to call churches to rediscover themselves as both within and *in-with* their neighborhood. That is to say, churches not only need to explore what it means to be within a particular place, but also how to collaborate in that place with others. They highlight four important challenges the church needs to embrace:

- The church WITHIN its specific local neighborhood
- The church IN-WITH Christians of different traditions for mutual flourishing
- The church WITHIN a definable place
- The church IN-WITH collaborating beyond its place[9]

They explain the difference this way:

> By *within* we mean standing in solidarity with your neighbors
> who have a shared desire to see your place be a good place to
> live. *Within* is about rooting within your context. . . . *In-with*
> is about collaborating in your neighborhood *with* others unto
> flourishing of life for all. *In-with* may be understood as a form
> of missional collaboration with others who also care about
> your place.[10]

Note how similar this approach is to the Emory model of social
change we explored earlier. For real social change to occur, people
need the self-awareness, integrity and empathy to be able to embrace
collaboration and common purpose with others. This is just as necessary in bringing change to the development of public places. The
fashioning of safe public spaces that catalyze community, equity and
relationship require collaboration among the city, urban planners,
architects, community groups, historic preservation societies and
more. It must take into account land use, local food systems, environmental sustainability, public health, transportation and more.
There's no question that the church can play a profoundly important
role, but it must recognize the need for deeper engagement and
greater cooperation with other voices in the city. Indeed, this is the
very work that God's midwives would perform because it creates
fertile spaces for God's new redemptive purposes to be birthed.

Churches can be dismissive of placecrafting as a missional enterprise because it seems more like community development work
rather than Christian mission. We would suggest that placecrafting
is essential for Christian mission. How can Christians meet their
neighbors or share their lives with them if the built environment
limits connection and proximity? Placecrafting is like watering a
garden or tilling a field. It creates the conditions for germination,
birth and growth to occur.

The Project for Public Spaces (PPS) has identified a number of principles for creating great community places.[11] While not a Christian organization, the key elements that PPS has come up with are entirely in keeping with missional practice. They are fantastically practical ideas for transforming parks, plazas, public squares, streets, sidewalks and other spaces into vibrant community places. Some of those elements are:

1. The neighborhood is the expert. I (Michael) regularly encourage church leaders to listen to their neighborhood. William Osler, one of the founding professors of Johns Hopkins Hospital, was noted to have said, "Listen to your patients, they are telling you the diagnosis." The diseased body "knows" what it needs, according to Osler, so if medical practitioners listen long enough and hard enough they will hear it. He established the full-time, sleep-in residency system, whereby doctors lived in the administration building of the hospital. A doctor could spend as long as seven or eight years as a resident, leading a restricted, almost monastic life devoted to healing their patients. We can't help but think that placecrafting requires the same kind of long-term devotion, listening to the heart of your community to discover its needs, as well as the talents and assets present within the community. As PPS says, "In any community there are people who can provide an historical perspective, valuable insights into how the area functions, and an understanding of the critical issues and what is meaningful to people."[12] Don't ignore these people. They are imperative to the process of placecrafting.

2. Craft a place, not a design. This involves introducing physical elements that help people feel welcome and comfortable, fostering a strong sense of community. Many older churches are situated right in the center of their towns and neighborhoods. What would it look like if such churches explored ways to open their properties to the community, by establishing herb gardens or providing public seating or playgrounds? Paul Ede, pastor of Clay Community Church in Glasgow, has a vision for the rehabilitation of unused public land around his area. Much of it has become a dumping ground for old tires and household rubbish. Kids fossick in the garbage piles and the area is an eyesore, and it's unsafe for smaller children. Through the establishment of community gardens, public greenspace and meadows, the church is helping to reshape the community at large, bringing greater dignity, amenity and utility to the spaces in his parish.

"Pop-up parks" are another fantastic example of what we're talking about here. These parks are cost-efficient, temporary spaces constructed in urban centers to cultivate a sense of community and enhance neighborhood ownership and identity. They are a brilliant example of what it looks like to innovate placecrafting beyond the megafunded built environment—to craft a place, not just a design. In 2014, East Village of downtown San Diego opened their first pop-up park, calling it simply the Quartyard: Your City Block. The idea started when three graduates from San Diego's New School of Architecture and Design identified an eyesore property across the street from their school, which inspired them to develop a thesis project to transform the unused land into something useful. They received a temporary lease for the land, put in fourteen shipping carts made from recycled and retrofitted materials, added some attractive landscaping and invited local food and business vendors to set up shop with a vision to build community together. The Quartyard hosts live music and film events, fundraisers, farmers and art markets and much more. Taking a vacant piece of property and activating the space with events and dining creates a deeper sense of community and pride in the East Village neighborhood of downtown San Diego.[13]

Innovative uses of land and buildings are going beyond good design to foster connectivity in cities that otherwise could remain cold and disconnected. This is a key element in placecrafting. It is within these kinds of initiatives that relationships are built and neighborhoods begin to contend for the greater good together.

3. Look for partners. As noted above, Sparks, Soerens and Friesen emphasize the need to be in-with a neighborhood, and this includes collaborating with like-minded neighbors. Such people are critical to the future success of a placecrafting project. A church might be able to start a community garden or refurbish a local park by themselves. But real success in making public spaces only occurs when the public are involved in planning, brainstorming, developing scenarios and implementation.

Many of our neighbors genuinely care about our shared place, whether they're actively involved in placecrafting efforts or not. And many are initiating brilliant placecrafting projects that we have much to learn from. To be clear, partnership like this is not a Christian strategy aimed at infiltrating our cities so that we, the church, can somehow take over or attempt to do things better. We need our neighbors in this venture! True partnership involves acknowledging and submitting to the skills, gifts and vision that already exist in our place. Celebrating the crafters of our wider community is part of what it means to fan the flame of what God is already doing in our place.

I (Christiana) was recently invited to participate in the beginnings of a city-wide event called the New Narrative, started by Nathan, not a Jesus follower, who lives in my neighborhood. Outside of his day job in public relations and marketing, Nathan is a speaking and writing coach who wanted to identify and gather local speakers and storytellers that he believes are making a significant difference in our city and around the world. He then puts on regular, open New Narrative events at local venues using various formats for public rhetoric. Nathan believes that storytellers can change society. If we can tell compelling, everyday, vulnerable stories, we can inspire each other to live differently, to feel a little less crazy and to believe that a new narrative for the future of our world is not only possibly but tangible.

Nathan invited me to join a discussion forum in preparation for a New Narrative event on community. Nathan had heard about our faith community in Golden Hill and was curious as to how we've seen intentional communities of faith in Jesus impact neighborhoods for good. I sat around the circle with incredible influencers from the public health field, local urban farmers, folks working to prevent ill treatment of undocumented immigrants, a radio host from a local station called El Daily Justice, a poet who uses his art to create awareness around issues of racism and discrimination in our city, and a nonprofit leader for local place-making. These discussions and public events are creating a stir in our city and binding people together to contend for peace and justice in our shared place.

We, the church, are to honor these partners, highlighting them, learning from them and working alongside them as we craft place together for the future we all long for.

4. You can see a lot just by observing. Juliet Kilpin from Urban Expression in the United Kingdom says we should reverse the old adage, "Don't just sit there, do something," to the more missional posture of, "Don't just do something, sit there!" Sit there. Take in your community. Observe what happens. Where are the nodes or the hubs in your neighborhood? Where do people congregate? Along what pathways do they move? A lot of church leaders are so desperate to start something, they launch new programs and schemes without ever truly observing their community.

Sean Benesh in Portland and Dennis Pethers in London each commend us to get up on the "rooftops" of our cities and metaphorically look down on them to observe how people live and move and find each other in such places.[14] In his book *The Space Between*, Eric

Jacobsen says, "It is important that we notice the space between the buildings because it is here where some of the more interesting things in life are likely to happen."[15] Or as the Project for Public Spaces puts it, "By looking at how people are using (or not using) spaces and trying to explore what they like and don't like about them, it is possible to assess what makes them work or not work."[16] Only through these kinds of meaningful observations can we be aware of what the reign of God could look like in our communities.

Walking through and observing your alleyways can tell you much more about the place than what is perhaps assumed. Alleys are the spaces where people go to be alone, to hide, to walk their dog, take a shortcut or just to keep a slower pace. Alleys are for concealed violence or secret love. Alleys express the unnoticed realities of our place. These hidden passageways need also to be factored into our practices of placecrafting. But without meaningful observing, we will never really see what we need to see behind the veneer. And this kind observing will compel us to purposeful action.

In our (Christiana's) neighborhood, there are all kinds of expressions of street art, some legal and some illegal. Especially in the alleyways, the messages that are posted, painted and plastered tell us more about our neighborhood than we are usually listening for. We can add our mark to these underlying messages through postings, tagging, stickers and even something as simple as chalk drawings. One of our community mates began to tag our neighborhood with the word "Kindness" as a mark of prayer drawn from the fruit of the Spirit in Galatians 5.

Placecrafting involves observing long enough to hear the subliminal messages of a culture and then creatively contributing our voice to shift, counteract or enhance what we, as a neighborhood, need to hear—the messages of God for our place.

5. Have a vision. The Project for Public Spaces encourages readers to have a vision, a plan that offers comfort, pride and beauty to the community. All good things. But our vision as followers of Christ is rooted in the reign of God. As Christopher Wright says, "Our mission is nothing less (or more) than participating with God in this grand story until he brings it to its guaranteed climax."[17] As followers of Christ, what is our distinctive vision for placecrafting? Where some placecrafting initiatives may end in experiences of fun, food and friendship, we believe the gospel intends something deeper, richer and more satisfying both for this life and the next. The ultimate end in God's coming kingdom changes the world at every level.

Placecrafting in the way of Jesus should always point us and others to the sending mission of Jesus recorded first in Isaiah 61 and repeated in Luke: "The Spirit of the LORD is upon me, for he has anointed me to bring Good News to the poor. He has sent me to proclaim that captives will be released, that the blind will see, that the oppressed will be set free" (Luke 4:18 NLT).

So how do *all* of our placecrafting ventures, big or small, finally direct us and others toward the restorative mission of God through Jesus? Placecrafting in the way of Jesus begins and ends with everyday faithfulness. Big vision is rooted in small acts of implementation. We usher in the opportunity for people not only to experience the redemptive reign of God but to enter into relationship with Christ in ways that bring freedom, restoration and healing, compelling them to contribute to the great vision of God for others as well.

Soon after Matt and Amy Chapman moved into their urban Seattle neighborhood they noticed a massive construction project underway at the heart of the main drag of their town. This particular building project was soon to hold a high-end grocery store with 193 luxury apartments layered on top. These rental apartments and the goods for sale underneath would not be affordable for many of the current neighborhood residents. This was a clear attempt by developers to change the economic tide of this neighborhood by raising the cost of living to attract those who could afford it. The Chapmans and their newly formed faith community called Common Life felt the strain alongside their neighbors. They began to pray for peace and creatively discern how to address this pending change. Stopping the oncoming train of gentrification is nearly impossible, but coming together as residents and linking arms to preserve the core values of a place can impact a neighborhood for good.

The Chapmans initiated a neighborhood-wide gathering at a local pub called Conversations that Matter and asked specific, long-time residents to sit on a panel to discuss the situation and give a broad perspective of how to best respond and band together as a community. They posted the event on the neighborhood Facebook page, which had over five thousand members. The Facebook post caused a stirring among neighbors who felt uncomfortable that a Christian group would facilitate a discussion of this nature. After an ongoing dialogue via Facebook, some highly respected older residents, not Christian, spoke up. Using Martin Luther King Jr. as a reference, they stated that "church groups and people of faith have instigated social change in positive ways throughout history and can be trusted for these kinds of initiatives." The neighborhood listened to their counsel, and a variety of residents expressed their support of a religious group hosting a neighborhood conversation so long as it remained inclusive.

This discussion forum provided a platform to hear from a diverse representation of neighborhood residents and from there to make conscious choices to look out for one another and walk forward in unity. From this one incident, a core group of neighbors are coming together to instigate initiatives of hope and change in their place.

6. *Money is not the issue.* It's tempting to think placecrafting only involves the development of expensive infrastructure or architectural design. In fact, as fun as it is to reimagine your city or town

completely redesigned, the chances are that's not going to happen. Working with the infrastructure of the public spaces, the elements that can be added to make it work (e.g., vendors, cafes, flowers and seating) will not be expensive. In addition, if you can mobilize the whole community and other partners the costs will be even lower. Placecrafting is far more meaningful when done at a grassroots level that requires everyone's simple participation for it to thrive. For example, installing a dog park depends on the dog owners to show up, interact, pick up after their dogs and keep the place as dog friendly as they can. Installing benches near public fountains with food trucks parked nearby simply depends on neighbors showing up to hang out, play games and take a lunch break. Placecrafting shouldn't be dependent on money or entertainment but on real people showing up in real places.

Children can help us understand this point because they don't need money to have fun, enjoy each other and be present to the moment. Give them trees, an open field, paper and scissors or an ice cream cone and they can enjoy it all! Children have the uncanny ability to imagine a larger reality in almost any circumstance. Consumerism draws us away from the heart of what placecrafting is meant to nurture. We must do our best to recover the simplicity of crafting a place that draws us together like children, able honor one another, enjoy the moment and imagine another future together.

7. *You are never finished.* The Project for Public Spaces says, "By nature, good public spaces that respond to the needs, the opinions and the ongoing changes of the community require attention. Amenities wear out, needs change and other things happen in an urban environment. Being open to the need for change and having the management flexibility to enact that change is what builds great public spaces and great cities and towns."[18]

We agree. It is an ongoing enterprise. I (Michael) have lived in the same neighborhood for fifty years. In that time I've seen regular changes, improvements and innovations sweep through our village. A town never gets to the point where its public spaces are finished.

As we noted earlier, placecrafting adds enormous value to a city. It's more than just a project in urban beautification. It attracts social capital, increases ecological diversity, adds cultural and economic vitality and generally enhances the quality of residents' lives. It has to be considered vital work for any Christians committed to bringing kingdom values and genuine cultural change to their neighborhoods.

10

BEING CHANGED AS WE BRING CHANGE

Everyone thinks of changing the world,
but no one thinks of changing himself.

LEO TOLSTOY

While we are certainly in agreement with the primary tenets of the missional conversation, we note that there hasn't been a lot of attention given to how our involvement in the redemptive mission of God actually alters us, the followers. If this way of life is the full expression of our identity, then in learning to follow the Spirit, emulate the Spirit and attend to what the Spirit is birthing around us, we will surely be changed. We have to be! As Paul writes, "And we all, who with unveiled faces contemplate the Lord's glory, are being transformed into his image with ever-increasing glory, which comes from the Lord, who is the Spirit" (2 Cor 3:18 NIV).

Much is lost when we only communicate the missional paradigm as something we achieve for others, forgetting that joining God's mission is a primary way for us to become who we were intended to be as well. In fact, it is critical that those of us who call ourselves missional people must examine every part of our lives under the lordship of Christ. The more authentically we embody mission the more we will be changed. Our truest life purpose can only flow out of who we are in the everyday incarnation of the mission of God within the place we inhabit. Some years ago, I (Michael) wrote a book with Alan Hirsch called *The Shaping of Things to Come.* Some readers might have thought it was a book about shaping the future, or shaping new church structures that would unleash missional energy. But all along we knew it was also a book about how mission shapes its participants.

Similarly, in their book *Missional Spirituality,* Roger Helland and Leonard Hjalmarson explore the all-encompassing nature of the missional life, both our acts and our inner life formation. They say, "We can't give what we don't have, and what we have to give is who we are. Christians must be real-life models of Christ's words and works. A missional spirituality is *fundamental to discipleship,* as Christ followers must become more like their Master, the founder and head of the church, the new humanity (Ephesians 2)."[1]

As we've shared in previous chapters, we believe that attending as God gives birth to the new creation requires a careful process of learning and practicing the ways of Jesus in our place. There are indeed ethics and limits to missionality as the Spirit leads us. To be real-life models of Christ's words and works in the world we mustn't forget that our inner formation is paramount. Who we are is not a sidebar to the missional life. Who we are *is* the missional life. Our ability to more faithfully join God, in the way of midwives, is hinged on whether or not we allow God to form us in the process. Jean Vanier, founder of the L'Arche communities around the world, writes,

Mission, then, does not imply an attitude of superiority or domination, an attitude of: "We know, you don't, so you must listen to us if you want to be well off. Otherwise you will be miserable." Mission springs necessarily from poverty and an inner wound, but also from trust in the love of God. Mission is not elitism. It is life given and flowing from the tomb of our beings which has become transformed into a source of life. It flows from the knowledge that we have been liberated through forgiveness; it flows from weakness and vulnerability. It is announcing the good news that we can live in humility, littleness and poverty, because God is dwelling in our hearts, giving us new life and freedom. We have received freely: we can give freely.[2]

EXPOSING OUR UNDERBELLIES

Webster's dictionary defines *underbelly* as "that which is vulnerable to attack—the dark, seamy and often hidden area." In a lot of missional literature we read of the call to enter into the underbellies of our cities, to engage the dark, seamy side of town, to serve the vulnerable and the broken. We echo these calls. We've pointed out the need to know your place, to expose its underbelly, to understand its pathologies and its history, to celebrate the good and to bring healing and restoration. Learning to identify and better understand these realities will instruct us on how to carefully love and contend in the way of Jesus in front of us. Mission involves making a commitment to be formed by God in our context, to learn to live interdependently in shared rhythms of life and to join the redemptive movements of God all around us.

God desires complete restoration. There is indeed a redemptive plan of God at play, inviting us to inhabit our place in the way of Jesus and join God's work of making all things new and just and whole. Yet, this inhabiting way of Jesus leads us not only to attend to the underbelly of our place but also to the underbelly of our inner life—to attend to the vulnerable, dark, seamy and often hidden area of our own being.

British poet and novelist Evelyn Underhill says, "We mostly spend [our] lives conjugating three verbs: to Want, to Have, and to Do. . . . We are kept in perpetual unrest: forgetting that none of these verbs have any ultimate significance, except so far as they are transcended by and included in, the fundamental verb, to Be: and that Being, not wanting, having, and doing, is the essence of a spiritual life."[3] The invitation to inhabit neighborhoods includes showing up with our whole heart, bringing our vulnerable selves to the surface and trusting God to form us more into the likeness of Christ.

Like many of you, I (Christiana) still ask myself the questions, *Am I doing enough? What if I fail? Do I even have what it takes?* I recently shared some of these anxious thoughts with Ben, a young barber and artist who lives across the street. In response to my questions, Ben pulled up the sleeve of his shirt and showed me his tattoo, which reads, "God saw fit to put poets in the world to invoke an unbridled pursuit of life." He explained that the world needs storytellers like me to invoke an unbridled pursuit of the meaning of life. "You need to tell the stories," he implored me.

I asked Ben if I could share his particular faith perspective. This is how Ben reflects on his own sense of spirituality: "That question always spins me. I'm an optimistic agnostic who practices meditation and prayer. Reason being, I haven't had a clear encounter with the God residing in Heaven yet. I have felt powers of the spirit, whatever they may be or wherever they may stem from, and I would really like to meet God one day. I suppose I'm a cheeky postmodernist. But I'm hopeful."

The prayer here is that both Ben and I would experience more tangible encounters with the living God in Jesus as we inhabit our place. This is what we mean by being changed by the mission to which God calls us. As we inhabit our place, we are encouraged in our work by people like my "optimistic agnostic" neighbor. That's how this life of attending as a midwife to what the Spirit is birthing in my place has altered the very underbelly of my life. This is a process, as Vanier says, where the tomb of my being is transformed into a source of life.

As I give myself more and more to the people to whom God has sent me I am being changed. Another such story is that of a woman named Roshel, who I met at a local coffee shop. Our friendly chit-chat turned into an hour-long conversation of uncovering our shared admiration for Jesus, our views on gender equality and our common experiences in intentional community. Roshel has a specific passion to advocate for women's rights around the world. She's also a member of an intentional humanitarian feminist community house that has been in our urban San Diego neighborhood for several years.

The next week Roshel invited me to her community house for tea. A big sign hung in the front window of the home that read, "Start Believing in Women," and in the front room there were portraits of historically influential women hanging on the wall. There was Dolores Huerta, a labor and civil rights activist who cofounded the National Farmworkers Association in the 1960s. And Frida Kahlo, the painter and activist whose work is celebrated in Mexico as a symbol of national tradition and pride for her uncompromising depiction of the female experience and form. And Rosie the Riveter, who said, "We can do it!," representing the voracious American women that worked in factories during World War II.

In the middle of the wall was a mirror. I caught a glimpse of my own reflection with the sun beaming down the side of my face. It was both enthralling and uncomfortable. Roshel put her hand on my shoulder, and with gentle smile, she said, "We've hung this mirror in the middle of these momentous paintings so that each of us can look deep into our own eyes and see the greatness within us." I could feel my vulnerabilities rising to the surface.

Roshel and I sat with the portraits, sipping our yerba mate tea. We spoke of the plight of women around the world in ways that made our hearts ache. Through tears, we told our own stories of disempowerment as women, and though we don't share the same faith convictions, my friend said, "We need to believe what Jesus said about women, about us." I could feel the gaze of these historical heroes and mentors awakening my dreams, validating my leadership and affirming my calling. And I could hear the voice of Jesus, advocating for my flourishing with the words, "I believe in you." God was attending to the vulnerabilities of my inner being.

As followers of Jesus in our neighborhoods, the Spirit will often guide us down unexpected routes of transformation. The process of our growth and revelation is not bound to the church building or structured places of theological training or spiritual enlightenment. Growth happens on the street, in the marketplace, in cafés, parks and homes. Growth can come in interactions with people of all different walks of life who share the place we call home.

The Holy Spirit is moving and speaking and birthing in our neighborhoods. As we learn to listen for the Holy Spirit at every turn, transformation may happen in the unforeseen moments of the sacred, ordinary, human-to-human life. Inhabiting our place begins by inhabiting ourselves, our own stories, as we are remade into the likeness of Christ through the mission of God.

COLABORERS WITH GOD

Just as God prunes our place for growth and restoration, so God prunes us. Many Christians are used to the idea that God uses our leaders to prune us. Through the ministries of teaching, correction, rebuke and encouragement we are held accountable, shaped and formed more into the likeness of Christ. We don't want to minimize these forms of pastoral ministry. But we'd like to add that one of the key ways God forms us is also via our engagement with the world in which we are placed. As God's colaborers in redemptive mission, it is our involvement in the lives of others that molds us according to the values of God's reign.

To return to a metaphor we used earlier, a midwife colabors with a birthing mother to usher new life into the world. In preparation for her work, the midwife carefully learns what each woman needs in order to thrive throughout her birth experience. A midwife travails side by side with a laboring mother, literally laboring with her—often moaning as she moans, swaying as she sways, offering her own body as a stabilizing presence to lean on, her shoulder to cry on and her hand to hold. These are vulnerable actions. And these are even more vulnerable when we accept that the Spirit is birthing something within us. We feel the pain, we embrace the pruning, we moan, we sway and stand firm with God until new life bursts out of us.

Colaboring is our mandate, our appointment and our responsibility within God's created order (Gen 1:29-30). We are invited to colabor in caring for God's world. God, the creator, is at work to redeem and restore all things, inviting us to join in as companions in the work. But let us not forget that we too are a part of this created order. As God births the new creation, we are not left out, exempt or on the sidelines of the restorative dream of God. The good news of Jesus is just as much for us as it is for our neighbor.

Just as the midwife comes alongside a birthing mother, so the Holy Spirit is inviting us, as colaborers, to work together with God in transforming even our own lives. This is a critical realization. If the life-giving mission of God isn't applied to our own inner formation, then we will never be able to step into our full vocation as colaborers of God. A midwife knows that every birth changes her, alters her very core and better equips her for the next birth.

Maxie and Chris Kamalski live in Cape Town, South Africa, with their young daughter, Mia. They are creating and nurturing a community of faith in their neighborhood, just walking distance from the Indian Ocean. Chris, a native Californian, and Maxie, from South Africa, live with deep conviction that inner life transformation is best worked out in slow, unglamorous ways through embedded, localized, contextualized relationships that form organically within a shared neighborhood. Chris, as a spiritual director and trainer, gives important insight to the inner work of God at play as we inhabit our place. He says, "In light of walking with God in ever deeper formation, I think of Paul's words in Philippians 2:12-13: 'Continue to work out your salvation with fear and trembling, for it is God who works in you to will and to act in order to fulfill his good purpose' [NIV]. There is a relational dynamic always at play between God and humanity. Our flourishing is birthed out of true companionship with the living God."[4]

This true companionship, or colaboring, is what ultimately sustains us for our calling in the birth of the new creation.

BEING ALTERED IN COMMUNITY

Inner life transformation happens in the crucible of community. Throughout Scripture the followers of God are urged to view themselves not as silos but as a part of an interdependent community. Interdependence draws out our best, our worst, our strengths and our weaknesses, reminding us that we cannot do this life alone. The metaphor of the body is used to describe the interconnected life of believers. Paul says in Romans 12:4-5, "Just as our bodies have many parts and each part has a special function, so it is with Christ's body. We are many parts of one body, and we all belong to each other" (NLT).

There isn't a one-size-fits-all format for the process of birth. In fact, there shouldn't be. Every birth is radically extraordinary. Birth locations, time frames, even the perspective of every midwife is uniquely different depending on their particular training, experience or personality. Within all these differences, however, there is a universal sentiment that applies to almost every birth event: no one was meant to give birth alone.

This path of interdependence, of being altered in community, isn't always an easy one to walk together. Modeling reconciliation and unity in the neighborhood, while universally recognized as important, is easier said than done. Social and ethnic divisions come with a long history of hurt and misunderstanding. So how do we become a reconciling presence in the places we inhabit while honoring the past and moving toward a unified vision for the future? Some of our best teachers are those from ethnic minority communities who've been practicing and modeling this kind of faithful presence for decades.

Pastor Michael Thomas of Radiant Church in the Skyway neighborhood of South Seattle is one such leader. As a church planter, Mike and his wife Kimberly had a vision to foster an authentically diverse community, held together in their differences by the unifying love of Jesus. Their church community is not only ethnically diverse but is also intergenerational, socio-economically spread, and represents contrasting political preferences and theological leanings. In a variety of ways, this church community regularly asks themselves, "How do we listen well to each other's story, learning to live together, centered on Jesus as our common denominator?"

A key component of leading a diverse community is to expect and welcome tension and discomfort. Mike says that intentionally identifying differences opens up more opportunity to explore the reconciling models that Jesus teaches. One story to illustrate this is a practice that Radiant Church calls Guess Who's Coming to Dinner. The title is taken from the 1967 film starring Sidney Poitier, Katharine Hepburn and Spencer Tracy about a young white woman introducing her African American fiancé to her parents over dinner. In a similar vein, Mike and Kimberly set up a night for the congregation to share meals around tables in homes, intentionally matching people up according to their differences.

They have to practice hospitality with one another, welcome one another into their homes and listen to one another's stories. As a result, friendships have developed with a deeper love and understanding of the unique differences that exist in their church community. These kinds of practices and slight deviations from what is commonly known as church fellowship have made for a beautifully diverse, caring and inclusive community of reconciliation.

The midwife leads and employs a birth community or team who will guard, protect and prepare for birth. There is much strategy involved in the leadership responsibilities of the midwife, just as there is in the process of attending God in the birth of the new creation. This role requires creative peacemaking, fierce contending and incredible self-sacrifice, all of which can apply beautifully to both the spiritual and physical realities that the followers of Jesus face every day.

Colaboring with God, leading and serving in community, midwifing what the Spirit is birthing around us and within us, involves a careful embodiment of practices that are drawn from the life, teachings and presence of Jesus fleshed out within a committed group of people. Jesus shows us that these practices are a communal expression, not a solo endeavor.

In 2002, Rob and Laurie Yackley started NieuCommunities, a ministry of CRM Empowering Leaders. After twenty years of international ministry with a calling to walk beside and develop Christian leaders for mission, the Yackleys noted that missionary teams or Christian communities had limited effectiveness and were susceptible to collapse because they did not know how to live well in community. As soon as things became difficult and conflict erupted, many would walk away, leaving their community with gaping wounds on both sides. Yet the Yackleys believed that the richest growth and the broadest impact for the redemption of God's world would happen as people learned to live in deep, Christ-centered community, joining the mission of God together.

With this enduring conviction, Rob and Laurie started Nieu-Communities as a network of mentoring and sending communities where young adults could be mentored, trained and equipped within the context of intentional communities of faith and reconciliation, embedded in neighborhoods around the world. Over the years, NieuCommunties staff identified six postures for creating and practicing missional community. These postures are both formational tools as well as ongoing sustainable practices for healthy communities who desire to commit together in inhabiting their place in the way of Jesus.

In their book *Thin Places: Six Postures for Creating and Practicing Missional Community*, Jon Huckins and Rob Yackley describe in detail the idea, story and learning behind these postures for creating and practicing missional community.[5] We'd like to briefly paraphrase their ideas as we ask the question of how to tangibly accept the invitation of God as colaborers in this work.

It is important to frame these six postures within three core commitments of the missional life. Drawn from the life and practice of Jesus, these commitments are: (1) communion with the triune God, (2) shared life in community with others and (3) a faithful, proactive engagement in the mission of God expressed in our common context. In short, that's communion, community and context. And we see these three commitments played out in Jesus' life and ministry. He was sent into his context with a purpose, intentionally surrounding himself with a band of disciples and sustained by the guidance of his heavenly Father. Likewise, we are sent into our context, strengthened by our interdependent life in community with others and sustained by our communion with the triune God.

Within this framework of communion, community and context, all of us, as we follow Jesus, can learn to walk through the six postures of missional formation, learning to faithfully live into our commitments and our collective calling. Those six postures are:

1. The listening posture. As we learn to become a people who are attuned to God, to community and to our shared place, we must be quick to listen and slow to speak, not assuming we know the answers or solutions but submitting ourselves to the God who leads us into the unknown as our teacher, our guide and our friend. We ask questions of God, of one another and of our context, listening long and deep for the Holy Spirit all around us.

2. The submerging posture. We posture ourselves as a people who courageously dive beneath the surface of our place to better understand before being understood and hear before being heard. Just as Jesus took on flesh, in a submerging posture we seek to become an integral part of our context with a desire to embody Jesus in all aspects of life.

3. The inviting posture. We posture ourselves as a people who creatively make room for others. We diligently seek to know and grasp the depths of God's invitation into kingdom living, becoming a more inviting and invited people and welcoming our neighbors into God's redemptive story.

4. The contending posture. We posture ourselves as a people who grapple with the rugged, transformative realities of what it means to follow the peacemaker Jesus in our context. This means we confront the things that hinder the full expression of the kingdom of God wherever we are, both spiritual and physical. We contend for peace and justice in our own souls, in our families, in our community, among our friends and neighbors, in our city and beyond.

5. *The imagining posture.* We posture ourselves to become a people who dream God's dreams at every turn. We cultivate prophetic imagination for what might or could be birthed in our place, with an ardent willingness to join God's work in seeing those dreams become reality. We desire to discern God's intent on our lives, in our communities and in our context.

6. *The entrusting posture.* We posture ourselves to hold people, places and plans loosely before our God who holds all things well. We learn to entrust these things to God, humbly accepting that our role in God's redemption story is only a chapter in a much greater story. We develop, empower and accompany others to carry on the work that God has started in us.

COMMUNITY IS HARD!

People sometimes talk about community in a way that makes it sound always easy and always beautiful. But actually it's difficult. Research shows that the number one reason why people give up on the missional life or choose to walk away from community is due to relational conflict. We get promised some big, warm, cozy sense of community and then we discover it's really tough to get along with one another. But surely God must have something spectacular in mind when we learn to live as reconciled and reconciling communities in our contexts. Imagine what a powerfully sacramental expression we could be as we live at peace with one another, fostering the peace of God in our place!

Yet peacemaking is no small matter. Conflict resolution is notoriously difficult, and for many people it can be terrifying. It requires deliberate wisdom, mature self-awareness and ardent courage. Moving forward in relational tension is not easy, but forward movement is the only path toward peace. Deep community cultivates the peace of God.

Conflict marks us with some of our deepest pain in life. It is also the pathway to some of our deepest transformation. As we've walked beside leaders who've left the church, stepped out of significant roles of influence, walked away from their faith or given up on God, we've found that almost always their decision to leave involves some sort of hurt from an unresolved conflict.

Living as communities in our neighborhoods in the way of Jesus necessitates conflict competency. We could tell story after story of our own successes and failures in the area of conflict resolution. Like the time when I (Christiana) reached the very end of my rope with someone in our community; we had toiled through differences and misunderstandings. As his community leader, I had spent many hours accommodating for our tension without directly facing the deeper issues. The pivotal moment for me was sitting with a mentor one summer afternoon and with tears in my eyes and boiling emotions, announcing, "Either I go or he goes. I can't do this with him anymore." I remember the look on my mentor's face as he gently called out my unwillingness to enter the tunnel of conflict with this brother and nudged me toward facing the situation head on. And I did. Though it was a ragged road forward it has been one of great redemption with significant implications for the health of our community.

The mission of God necessitates that we enter our contexts in community. And community necessitates that we regularly toil through the conflict in our lives. And conflict resolution changes us and others. You can't do missional community and not be changed by it. Perhaps that's why Jesus said, "So if you are presenting a sacrifice at the altar in the Temple and you suddenly remember that someone has something against you, leave your sacrifice there at the altar. Go and be reconciled to that person. Then come and offer your sacrifice to God" (Mt 5:23-24 NLT).

The strength of our inner life, the health of our community and the ministry that God has called us to are hinged on the reality of our faithful movement toward reconciliation in the small, ordinary, everyday relationships of our lives. If we are to lead communities who follow the way of Jesus, joining God's mission of reconciliation in the catastrophic conflicts of our world, we must first practice peacemaking in our day-to-day, human-to-human relationships. We must learn to live as reconciling communities at every possible level.

In his book *Unexpected Gifts: Discovering the Way of Community*, Chris Heuertz names the realities that most often destroy a community—things such as failure, disagreement, transition, betrayal, lack of self-awareness, grief and incompatibility, to name a few. Heuertz shares his learning from more than twenty years of living in intentional Christian community, describing how the very things they thought would destroy community actually became their greatest gifts, leading to a discovery of what he would call "the true way of community."

Heuertz offers a blessing prayer, an anthem of faith, encouraging readers to allow their "lives to be woven together to create vibrant tapestries of hope." This journey of inhabiting neighborhoods in the way of Jesus as communities of reconciliation is a journey that many will desire and yet few will embark upon. Yet the challenge is worth proclaiming over and over. For this is an invitation to life as it was meant to be lived.

> Let our failures further unite us, illuminating the
>   hidden beauty within us.
> May our doubts lead to greater faith.
> Let us never become so isolated that we lose the fragrance
>   of the blossoms
>   under our very noses.
> May isolation expose our divisions and lead us to healing
>   and wholeness.

Let our transitions be grace-filled, accepting, and honest.
May we come to truly know ourselves, receiving the beauty
and terror of our humanity.
Let our love not lead to betrayal.
May we find better ways to negotiate chemistry and
compatibility without
losing one another or ourselves along the way.
Let our gratitude by sustained, leading us away from
unspoken resentments.
May we never forget to celebrate, even as we grieve.
May we live faithfully in the undramatic—the incubator of
our imaginations—
bearing witness to hope . . .
And in discovering the unexpected gifts of shared space, live
the way of community.[6]

11 SUFFERING ALONG THE WAY

*Vulnerability is the birthplace of innovation,
creativity and change.*

BRENÉ BROWN

We began by suggesting that, like exiles in Babylon, the church today finds itself in a seemingly foreign land. The culture that Christians once had so much influence on is changing. The ground appears to be slipping out from under us. The world seems broken beyond repair, and our hearts grieve for the suffering and the bewildered in our midst. Like the Hebrew exiles we find ourselves questioning where God is and what God is doing.

But we also began this book by restating the firm conviction all Christians can share: that Christ has triumphed over sin, death and despair and God is leading history toward its true end. As Lesslie Newbigin wrote, "The Church in each place is to be the sign, instrument and foretaste of the reign of God present in Christ."[1] So we have attempted to explore the way the church can be midwives to the ongoing birth of the new creation. And we've seen the need for the church to embrace the following challenges:

- Enter society as a potentially disruptive presence.
- Suspend prefabricated agendas and follow the opportunities as God presents them.
- Open the space in which God is working by taking the context very seriously.
- Remain flexible and adaptable, following the cues of the Spirit.
- Live out a viable and appealing alternative reality to the world around us.
- Embrace the necessary collaboration to affect change in every level of society.
- Equip Christians to be change agents in every vocation.
- Fashion public places that foster the values of the kingdom.
- Be humble enough to be changed by your context while also bringing change.

The mission of God invites us to enter—fully enter—into neighborhood and into community, and both come with a cost. When our presence in a city brings changes there can be opposition. We have spoken of incarnational witness in a city, of altering the nature of our work, and of placemaking as though they are straightforward matters. But whenever we bring changes to a context we will upset the preexisting stasis, and that can bring disapproval or even hostility from those who are happy with the status quo. Remember Paul in Ephesus? He evoked a riot. Indeed, an exploration of Paul's ministry as described in Acts 19 is an interesting case study in Christian mission.

At that time Ephesus was dominated by the colossal marble statue of the goddess Artemis. Pilgrims and tourists came from across the known world to gaze upon the structure and worship within its white stone walls. Ephesus's economy had become increasingly dependent on trade associated with the cult of Artemis. Tradesmen made their living supplying visitors with religious trinkets, along with offerings and lodging.

Into this religious and economic landscape came the apostle Paul, preaching the gospel of Jesus. He planted a congregation in Ephesus on his second mission tour in AD 52. A couple of years later he returned and settled down to conduct his ministry there for over two years, possibly as long as three years. Luke wrote: "God did extraordinary miracles through Paul, so that when the handkerchiefs or aprons that had touched his skin were brought to the sick, their diseases left them, and the evil spirits came out of them" (Acts 19:11-12). The Greek words for "handkerchiefs" and "aprons" could refer to Paul's own sweatbands and the garments he wore when making tents for a living. In a city that lived in the grip of religious mania, these stories were astonishing. While the local sorcerers relied on convoluted recipes and incantations, and charged highly for their services, Paul's dirty work clothes were used to heal the sick, and at no cost. After Paul triumphed in a public showdown with the seven sons of Sceva the sorcerer, many locals renounced their beliefs in sorcery and burned their scrolls of magic incantations.

Acts 19:10 states: "All the residents of Asia, both Jews and Greeks, heard the word of the Lord." For all this activity to be conducted under the very nose of the statue of Artemis in her astonishing temple is nothing short of remarkable.

It is tempting to imagine that all this progress was achieved without drama. But we know otherwise. Indeed, the reaction to the success of Paul's ministry by local business leaders was one of the most dramatic experiences of his life.

A man named Demetrius, probably the leader of a regional guild of silversmiths, called together not only his own guild but also those in related trades. Paul's work, and the growth of the church in Ephesus, was having an effect on the industry in religious paraphernalia. Demetrius's mob wanted to rid the city of Paul and his corrupting influence. Paul had not only offended their religious faith, but also had disturbed powerful vested business interests.

The protestors began chanting, "Great is Artemis of the Ephesians!" This attracted other people, and before long the entire city was in an uproar. In the frenzy, two Christians, friends of Paul named Gaius and Aristarchus, were manhandled into the amphitheater, where they faced uncertain danger. Paul's first instinct was to join them, to protect his associates and perhaps turn the mood of the crowd with some oratory, but he was dissuaded from entering the theater by, of all people, the city officials who didn't want the spectacle of a brutal lynching happening on public property.

Fearful that in their religious mania the tradesmen might confuse them with the Christians, Alexander, the leader of the local Jewish community, entered the theater in order "to make a defense before the people" (Acts 19:33). Jews had lived in an uneasy peace with the worshipers of Artemis for generations. No doubt Alexander wanted to explain this to the crowd and distance himself and his community from the troublemaking Christian sect. In any case, he was shouted down and the theater erupted in frenzied cries of "Great is Artemis of the Ephesians!" for about two hours.

In the end the riot was quelled by the city officials. They managed to extract the hapless Gaius and Aristarchus from the theater and convince the mob they were no threat to their business. They also successfully explained that any regress the tradesmen felt toward Paul should be presented as evidence in a court of law, not by chanting in a wild demonstration. "For we are in danger of being charged with rioting today, since there is no cause that we can give to justify this commotion" (Acts 19:40). This was a veiled threat that the might of Rome could come down on the city if it was deemed to be lawless.

MISSION IS SUFFERING

The story of Paul's ministry in Ephesus is a perfect case study in the dangers and challenges of incarnational culture-altering mission. The city of Ephesus was a delicately poised arrangement of civic and sacred activities. The rioting tradesmen were concerned for the free and unfettered conduct of *both* their business and religious interests. Only Western readers can think that the Ephesus rioters were merely outraged trade unionists grousing about the effect on their incomes of Paul's activities. They were devout followers of the cult of Artemis, against which the claims of Jesus stood in stark relief. Ephesian society was like a house of cards, each one deftly balanced against the others. Add one more card to the structure and the whole house comes tumbling down. And that's exactly what Paul's arrival in Ephesus did. Introducing a new element to an already delicately poised society upset the balance.

In chapter three we pointed out that followers of Christ will alter any system they make an effort to truly enter. The changes they bring can be appreciated and valued, or they can be rejected. The situation in Ephesus is an example of the latter. In most neighborhoods it will be a mix of welcome and rejection. If we decide to run a feeding program the poor might welcome it, while the local shopkeepers and small business owners might reject us for bringing a "bad element" into the area. Michael visited a church in Mobile, Alabama, that built a low-cost gym on their property for the use of their community, but had to restrict its membership when some patrons started using the parking lot for various nefarious activities, frightening the church's closest neighbors.

Likewise, a church in Newcastle, England, started handing out free pancakes to drunken patrons of the local pubs as they were walking home late on Saturday nights. The rationale for this exercise was to put food in the alcohol-filled bellies of revelers and to share the gospel with them. They thought their neighbors would value this ministry, but the local fish-and-chip and kebab shop owners were furious that they were being put out of business and petitioned the council to stop the church.

Earlier we mentioned the example of Ed, the Northern California school administrator who, as a direct result of his Christian convictions, has been involved in seeking to revitalize a number of dysfunctional or dying schools across his region. The families in these towns have been delighted that these schools are being rejuvenated, as are small business owners, because healthy schools contribute to healthier neighborhoods. But the teachers' unions have been infuriated by Ed's work because it has meant changed work agreements and salaries and the removal of incompetent teachers.

It is important that churches do as much research and cultural exegesis as they can to try to avoid making these kinds of blunders. But there are often factors no one could ever predict. As a result, we have Paul's conflict with the silversmiths, potters and stonemasons of Ephesus. Churches committed to truly entering incarnationally into their neighborhoods have to recognize there will be a cost to pay. As Ajith Fernando from Youth for Christ in Sri Lanka writes, "If the apostle Paul knew fatigue, anger, and anxiety in his ministry, what makes us think we can avoid them in ours?"[2]

What we are talking about is the need to *contextualize* our ministries effectively. The shorthand definition of contextualization is "so presenting Jesus to a context that he causes offense for the proper biblical reasons, not the wrong cultural ones." Churches need to develop the skills to analyze their contexts and shape their ministry responses accordingly. But never imagine you can live an opposition-free life in following Jesus. As theologian René Padilla put it:

> Christian mission and Christian discipleship are two sides of the same coin. Both derive their meaning from Jesus, the

crucified Messiah, who even as Lord remains crucified. The Christian mission is the mission of those who have identified themselves with the Crucified and are willing to follow him to the cross. Mission is suffering.[3]

It would be irresponsible of us to call you to embrace the culture-altering work of following Jesus into the world without warning you that it could very well result in misunderstanding, suspicion and even out-and-out opposition.

I (Michael) was recently discussing this very point with a minister in California. He tried to dismiss me casually by saying, "You write about being missional, don't you? What is that exactly? Being a friendly neighbor and starting community gardens?" Not daunted by his disdain, I attempted a serious explanation, before he pressed the matter by describing missional people as just wanting to hang out in the neighborhood, drink beer, volunteer at homeless shelters, complain about traditional churches, "read fancy books and discuss Coen brothers films." He was obviously annoyed at what he saw as a kind of loosey-goosey approach to church that involved no organization and no real engagement with the kind of evangelistic enterprise that might offend our neighbors. Did he have a point? Recently David Fitch posted a question on social media: "By and large, most missional churches are simply Sunday services with some justice projects added on. Agree?" If this is all the missional conversation has led to, then we think it's a great reduction of all missional theology seeks to explore. If all this new thinking does is to get existing churches to commit to the occasional justice-oriented "add-on," it's been a failure. We strongly suspect that behind this reductionist approach to mission is a fear that many new church leaders have of offending their neighbors. They've seen the ways previous generations of church people have annoyed their neighbors by being obnoxious, judgmental or just plain socially weird. We wonder whether there's been an oversteering back in the other direction, toward an apprehension about ever treading on anyone's toes.

In saying this, we are not encouraging you to go looking for trouble. Paul clearly didn't. As we hope we've made clear, missional Christians need to enter their contexts in community with listening ears and wide eyes. But there are times when we can't avoid the suffering that comes from standing with the redemptive purposes of God.

Indeed, this is why we are anxious about the approach of Christian Dominionism we mentioned earlier. The idea of "conquering" society, or claiming dominion over the various elements of our culture, is the opposite of the midwifing characteristics we've discussed—suspending our agendas, holding space, being adaptive. When Christian leaders go on national television and claim that a military takeover is needed to reclaim our country for Christ, we are far from the community of the Suffering Servant we were meant to be. It's simply not biblical to claim that it is our duty to take dominion over all aspects of society in order for the kingdom to come on earth. The kingdom *has* come. And it *is* coming. And our role is to be willing to suffer to support its unfurling wherever God may send us. Such suffering may come in the form of persecution (and here we mean real persecution, not just the mockery of sharp-tongued TV hosts), or it might simply come in the form of the heartache of loving the unloved and serving the needy.

TO SUFFER THE HEARTACHE OF LOVING TOO MUCH

Dr. Mark Seltzer tells the story of doing his rounds as a medical registrar in a busy hospital and passing the room of a terminally ill young woman. Her husband, who was seated by her bed holding her hand, looked up as Dr. Seltzer glanced in.

"Is there anything I can do?" the doctor asked politely, knowing there was in fact nothing to be done.

"Yeah," the young husband replied, "remind me never to love this much again."

To love this broken world with the love of Christ will lead to heartache and grief. We will suffer not only from the slings and arrows of those who would resist our efforts, but we will necessarily suffer the pain of loving and losing others. On the other side of pain is love.

My (Christiana's) neighbor, Lola, was a tremendous woman of resilience, wisdom and creativity. She affected our community in lasting ways. We met Lola stranded on the sidewalk where her electric wheelchair had broken down. As we helped her get back to her apartment, Lola wrote down her phone number on a tiny piece of paper and said in her snarky way, "Don't be a stranger!" Over the years we built a deep and trusting friendship with Lola, a friendship that taught us much about the cost of truly loving our neighbors.

Lola lived in an independent-living complex for at-risk and houseless seniors with mental health issues or dual diagnoses. She gardened in our backyard, joined us for meals and holidays, and attended our regular hangouts in the park. Our friendship was a beautiful mess of giving and receiving, joy and strain. I remember a time when Lola called to ask if I would pick up a prescription from the pharmacy and bring it to her apartment as soon as possible. It was a Friday evening and I was all dressed up, ready to head out the door for a birthday dinner party.

Grudgingly I arrived at Lola's door. I'd been in this position with her countless times before and, frankly, I was impatient. Lola wheezed with labored breath as she explained how in addition to her bronchial infection she had misplaced the primary tube to connect to her breathing machine. In my party wear, I got down on my hands and knees, pulling things out from under Lola's bed. My irritation increased. Then I glanced over at Lola's bare feet, dangling from her wheelchair, dirty, swollen and calloused. I remembered in that moment my calling as a disciple of Jesus to wash my neighbors' feet—to symbolically serve them with sacrificial love in a way that expresses the tangible presence of God, not just once but over and over and over again.

After a few minutes of hunting, I found the tube wrapped in a soiled blanket on her bed. As Lola started to breathe rhythmically again, I placed my hand on her chest and prayed for the healing breath of God to flow through her lungs. Under her breath I heard Lola whisper, "Thank you."

There was another time when Lola asked, "Am I your project?" My heart sank. Her question pierced me. Lola challenged me to examine my deepest motivations in learning to love my neighbor. She was not my project. She was my friend.

When Lola died in 2014, it was Rebecca, a member of our community, who found her. Later the police called me as Lola's next of kin. She was estranged from any family and her adoption into our community for the last five years of her life was the closest thing to family she had known in decades. We hosted Lola's memorial service in our backyard. Our community thanked God with tears in our eyes for the privilege of knowing Lola, learning what it means to live as family in this world, beyond social barriers.

Lola was a gift to us. Her stories, her wisdom, the harvest from her garden and her piercing questions were a source of life to our community. We suffered with her and for her. God's altering work of love in our place is just as much about our formation, through suffering and love, as it is about the mission out in front of us. Perhaps God will form us through our family, faith community or friends. Or maybe God will form us through an elderly wise sage who commutes around town in an electric wheelchair, such as Lola. But one thing we can be certain of is this: it will involve heartache.

TO SUFFER THE DISAPPOINTMENT OF LIMITED RESULTS

I (Michael) have a friend named Greg Hunt who leads Paseo Christian Church in El Paso, Texas. The community of Paseo lives among and serves the houseless and the poor of downtown El Paso, not far from the mighty Rio Grande. Greg loves his community deeply and enjoys seeing the reign of God unfold in the dark corners of his city. But recently, in conversation with a well-meaning pastor, his church was described as "underperforming." At first that stung Greg. Previously, he had been part of a highly successful church-planting network associated with a megachurch up north. He was used to their metrics for assessing the performance of churches—numbers, money, baptisms. He knew that according to such measures Paseo was certainly underperforming. Being seen that way by his friend, and possibly imagining the chorus of other pastors and church planters who might see his work as substandard, Greg felt the humiliating pain of being judged a failure. His is a common experience for many who follow the call of God to work as midwives in the hard places of the world.

And yet, as Greg thought more about it and looked at the evidences of the reign of God flowering in the soil of Paseo, he had a change of heart. He thought about Chuck, a formerly houseless man who is now midwifing a beautiful expression of God's reign in El Paso. Chuck had started showing up to one of Paseo's gatherings, and as the months unfolded, went from eating all the free donuts to bumming a few bucks from Greg to asking if the church could put him up in a hotel because he couldn't stand it at the shelter where he felt unsafe. Paseo slowly became his family.

Chuck doesn't have a high school diploma and has physical limitations, so work is hard to come by. Enter Jorge the realtor. Jorge became friends with Chuck, inviting him into community, hanging out with him on the streets and helping him find jobs here and there. One day, Jorge brokered a deal for an apartment complex in downtown El Paso, a few blocks from Paseo's gathering location. Part of the deal was that Chuck would be the super. And it worked. Chuck was no longer without a house, and he had a job he loved.

Now Chuck wants to do for others what Jorge did for him. So he's linked up with a guy named Neill Trull, Paseo's missional community catalyst, and started putting together a plan. A community has sprung up on Wednesday afternoons where Jesus, jobs and getting clean is discussed and prayed over. Chuck and Neill have made a connection between a few temp agencies, and an impromptu clothes closet has started in Chuck's apartment where people can access clothes that could be worn to a job interview. As Greg writes, "Chuck the homeless guy who can pound a whole box of donuts in about thirty minutes is now leading a movement. I don't know what is gonna happen, but I'm glad I'm along for the ride. And Paseo underperformed this much. Because if this is underperforming, I'll take it."

But it's hard to get to that point. The success culture in our churches insists we "perform" in conventionally measurable ways. How do you measure Chuck's story? Being willing to suffer the negative assessments of others will inevitably be the lot of those who follow God into mission. Also, we need to be willing to see that even when things aren't going so well in our churches God could still be hard at work.

There is often a pause in the second stage of labor, just as a baby is about to be born. Midwives call it "the time to rest and be thankful." It is a moment when a birthing mother catches her breath, gathers her strength and waits in gratitude for the final rush. As God is birthing new things in our lives and in our world there is often a pause before the final stretch, a clearing or a stillness before new life emerges. It is a gift and a sign of the coming renewal of Christ. Sometimes the slowness or dryness our churches experience as we embed in our contexts is just that—not a sign of death, but a pause before the bursting forth of new life.

Jodi Hansen is the executive director of an affiliate of Love INC, an organization that helps networks of pastors and churches engage in neighborhood mission. She also had a career as labor and delivery nurse. When we mentioned our metaphor of God birthing the new creation and the church acting as midwives in its delivery, Jodi offered an important insight. She said that when labor slows down in the Western hospital context, we don't often wait for progress. We medicate, anesthetize, urge the mother to push harder, then intervene with every method we can muster to speed the delivery along. And if none of that works, medical staff quickly resort to performing a cesarian section. While there are certainly critical times when cesarians are necessary, more commonly, waiting for a woman's body to do what it needs to do in this stage of labor is considered too inefficient and tedious. "It sounds like the church is similar," Jodi says. "When things seem slow in our churches, we fire and hire, we push harder, we shut things down and change things up, all in an attempt to restart growth. Yet the pause might actually have been God's needed intention."

TO SUFFER THE ACHE FOR A NEW WORLD

The author of *The Epistle of Mathetes to Diognetus*, writing in the second century, described the early Christians this way,

> They dwell in their country, but simply as sojourners. As citizens, they share in all things as if foreigners. Every foreign land is to them as their native country and every country of their birth as a land of strangers. They marry as do all others; they beget children; but they do not destroy their offspring. They have a common table, but not a common bed. They are in the flesh, but do not live after the flesh. They pass their days

on earth, but they are citizens of heaven. They obey the pre-
scribed laws, and at the same time surpass the law by their
lives. They love all men and are persecuted by all. They are
unknown and condemned; they are put to death and restored
to life; they are poor, yet make many rich; they are in lack of
all things and yet abound in all; they are dishonored and yet
in their very dishonor they are glorified. They are evil spoken
of, and yet are justified; they are reviled and bless; they are
insulted, and repay the insult with honor; they do good, yet
are punished as evil doers. When punished, they rejoice as if
quickened into life; they are associated by the Jews as for-
eigners and are persecuted by the Greeks; yet those who hate
them are unable to assign any reason for their hatred.[4]

The early Christians changed the monstrous Roman Empire by literally eating away at its foundations, wooing simple, everyday people
with a vision and an example of the world to come in Christ. This is
how you change your world—by infiltrating every part of it and living
out the values of God's reign despite persecution or misunderstanding.
Today we need to find a fresh unction of courage. Not the kind of
courage that wants to antagonize our detractors or stir up opposition,
but the kind of reckless courage required to live as those second-
century Christians did. To *ache* with desire for a world made whole.

For what we Christians often lack is not the right theology or the
right strategy. We lack a holy dissatisfaction with the world as it is.
Yearning—truly yearning—for justice and mercy is a kind of suffering. To lament and be brokenhearted at racism and misogyny
and senseless murder and the madness of militaries—these things
come with a cost. They are burdensome. And it often feels as though
it is a burden not shared by enough of us.

In 1912, General William Booth, founder of The Salvation Army,
entered Royal Albert Hall in London to address a gathering of

7,000 Salvationists, a faithful army of his followers. It would be his final sermon, and it perfectly described not only his own ministry but also the mission of his beloved Salvation Army:

> While women weep, as they do now, I'll fight; while children go hungry, as they do now I'll fight; while men go to prison, in and out, in and out, as they do now, I'll fight; while there is a poor lost girl upon the streets, while there remains one dark soul without the light of God, I'll fight, I'll fight to the very end![5]

Today he might have added to fight against the ravaging of God's earth, and the destruction of God's world; to fight against the murder of children, and death of refugees at sea; to fight against police brutality and the building of walls to stop the poor; to fight injustice and inequity and to fight being labeled socialists for doing so. Just three months after delivering that sermon, William Booth was dead at the age of eighty-three. His fight had ended, his burden lifted.

Another fighter for justice was the Danish playwright and pastor Kaj Munk. A member of the Danish resistance against Nazi occupation during World War II, Munk wrote a powerful ode to holy rage. In part it reads, "To rage at the senseless killing of so many and against the madness of militarism. To rage at the lie that calls the threat of death and the strategy of destruction 'peace.' To rage against complacency of so many in the church. . . . To restlessly seek that recklessness which will challenge, and to seek to change human history until it conforms to the norms of the kingdom of God. . . . The signs of the Christian church have always been the lion, the lamb, the dove and the fish. But *never* the chameleon."[6]

We've already noted that it's not our rage or our fight that changes the world. That is entirely the work of God. But we share the words of Kaj Munk, who was murdered by the Nazis in 1944, and those of General Booth because they illustrate the burdensome yearning

of those who crave a world made right. It was a burden carried by
the exiles in Babylon as well. They were encumbered with a pal-
pable desire for their freedom. And so God gave Isaiah another
vision of their future, a picture of their world made right again.
Speaking to a bowed and broken nation of slaves, men and women
described as a cluster of grapes with just a drop of juice left in them
(Is 65:8), Isaiah paints a picture of all they've hoped for. He dreams
of a restored Jerusalem, the perfected city:

> "Never again will there be in it
>   an infant who lives but a few days,
>   or an old man who does not live out his years;
> the one who dies at a hundred
>   will be thought a mere child;
> the one who fails to reach a hundred
>   will be considered accursed.
> They will build houses and dwell in them;
>   they will plant vineyards and eat their fruit.
> No longer will they build houses and others live in them,
>   or plant and others eat.
> For as the days of a tree,
>   so will be the days of my people;
> my chosen ones will long enjoy
>   the work of their hands.
> They will not labor in vain,
>   nor will they bear children doomed to misfortune;
> for they will be a people blessed by the Lord,
>   they and their descendants with them.
> Before they call I will answer;
>   while they are still speaking I will hear.
> The wolf and the lamb will feed together,
>   and the lion will eat straw like the ox,

and dust will be the serpent's food.
They will neither harm nor destroy
  on all my holy mountain,"
    says the Lord. (Is 65:20-25 NIV)

This is our dream also. The dream of a new heaven and a new earth, the world to which God is giving birth. This is the world that we have graciously and generously been invited to midwife into existence. God, groaning and crying out, like a woman in labor, is birthing the new creation before our very eyes. As we join God in the delivery, we embrace the reality that we cannot birth the new world with our own efforts and achievements. Rather, as God births, we attend, like midwives, always learning, always in awe, always changed. This is how Jesus alters the world.

ACKNOWLEDGMENTS

We would like to acknowledge the support and hard work of our editor, Helen Lee, who not only helped shape the overall structure of this book, but also contributed to its content by pushing us to engage with ideas that have enhanced the quality of our work. We also want to thank Cindy Bunch from IVP for her support for our work, and for taking a risk on a project that started out as a book by a single author and soon turned into a coauthored book involving a novice writer. That took great trust on her part, and we're very grateful.

Michael: I would like to acknowledge the continued support of Morling College for allowing me the space to research and write, as well as the freedom to travel and engage with missional practitioners around the globe.

Christiana: I would like to thank my neighbors, friends and family who've cheered me on in this writing venture. Thank you to Rob Yackley, my colleague and mentor with Thresholds, for investing in my development as a missional voice and practitioner. Thanks to my parents, Toni and Rick Chase, for embodying the deep joy of following Christ in the complexities of our world. And to my daughters, Naomi and Anika, for their wild wonder and curiosity that stretches my imagination every day. And especially to Derek, my life companion, for believing in me with enduring love as we attend to God in the birth of the new creation.

NOTES

1 GOD GROANS LIKE A WOMAN IN LABOR

[1]Lesslie Newbigin, *The Open Secret: An Introduction to the Theology of Mission*, rev. ed. (Grand Rapids: Eerdmans, 1995), 33-34.

[2]N. T. Wright, *The Challenge of Jesus: Rediscovering Who Jesus Was and Is* (Downers Grove, IL: InterVarsity Press, 1999), 184.

[3]Rakesh Kochhar and Richard Fry, "Wealth Inequality Has Widened Along Racial, Ethnic Lines Since End of Great Recession," December 12, 2014, www.pewresearch.org/fact-tank/2014/12/12/racial-wealth-gaps -great-recession.

[4]Ed Stetzer, "A Decision in Ferguson: How Should Evangelicals Respond?," *The Exchange: A Blog by Ed Stetzer, Christianity Today*, November 24, 2014, www.christianitytoday.com/edstetzer/2014/november/decision -in-ferguson-how-should-evangelicals-respond.html.

[5]Leonce Crump, "It's Time to Listen: Will White Evangelicals Ever Acknow- ledge Systemic Injustice? (Part 2)," *The Exchange: A Blog by Ed Stetzer, Christianity Today*, August 22, 2014, www.christianitytoday.com/edstetzer /2014/august/its-time-to-listen-will-white-evangelicals-ever-acknowledge .html.

[6]Stetzer, "A Decision in Ferguson."

[7]Michelle Alexander, *The New Jim Crow: Mass Incarceration in the Age of Colorblindness* (New York: The New Press, 2012), 258.

[8]See heedinggodscall.org/content/pfctoolkit-10.

[9]Amy Roberts and Lindsey Knight, "By the Numbers: Memorial Day and Veterans," May 26, 2016, www.cnn.com/2012/05/25/politics/numbers -veterans-memorial-day.

[10]For statistics on domestic violence, see Soraya Chemaly, "50 Facts About Domestic Violence," January 30, 2013, www.huffingtonpost.com/soraya -chemaly/50-actual-facts-about-dom_b_2193904.html.

[11]Alan Yuhas, "One in 30 US Children Are Homeless as Rates Rise in 31 States, Report Finds," November 17, 2014, www.theguardian.com/us -news/2014/nov/17/report-one-in-30-us-children-homeless.

[12]Lawrence B. Finer and Mia R. Zolna, "Declines in Unintended Pregnancy in the United States, 2008–2011," March 3, 2016, *The New England Journal of Medicine*, www.nejm.org/doi/full/10.1056/NEJMsa1506575.

[13]Carlos Rodriguez, "Jennifer Lawrence Challenges the Church," *My Christian Daily*, January 21, 2016, mychristiandaily.com.au/dr/jennifer -lawrence-challenges-the-church. Emphasis added.

[14]Ibid.

[15]Rod Dreher, "Orthodox Christians Must Now Learn to Live as Exiles in Our Own Country," *Time*, June 26, 2015, time.com/3938050/orthodox -christians-must-now-learn-to-live-as-exiles-in-our-own-country/.

[16]Mark Woods, "Gay Marriage Is Legal in the US. Try Not to Worry," *Christian Today*, June 26, 2015, www.christiantoday.com/article/gay .marriage.is.legal.in.the.us.try.not.to.worry/57286.htm.

[17]David Brooks, "The Next Culture War," *New York Times*, June 30, 2015, www.nytimes.com/2015/06/30/opinion/david-brooks-the-next-culture -war.html.

[18]David J. Bosch, *Transforming Mission* (Maryknoll, NY: Orbis, 1991), 515.

[19]Elizabeth Achtemeier, "Exchanging God for 'No Gods,' A Discussion of Female Language for God," *Theology Matters* 12, no. 3 (May/June 2006): 2.

[20]Elizabeth Johnson, *She Who Is* (New York: Crossroad Publishing, 2002), 55.

[21]Achtemeier, "Exchanging God," 4.

[22]Walter Brueggemann, *The Word Militant* (Minneapolis: Augsburg Fortress, 2010), 143.

2 WHAT'S STANDING IN OUR WAY?

[1]N. T. Wright, *Simply Christian: Why Christianity Makes Sense* (London: SPCK, 2006), 236.

[2]N. T. Wright, *Surprised by Hope* (New York: HarperCollins, 2008), 265.

[3]Christena Cleveland, "Urban Church ~~Planting~~ Plantations," March 18, 2014, www.christenacleveland.com/2014/03/urban-church-plantations.
[4]Ibid.
[5]Paul Sparks, Tim Soerens and Dwight J. Friesen, *The New Parish* (Downers Grove, IL: InterVarsity Press, 2014), 90.

3 A DIVINE DISRUPTION

[1]Carolyn Sharp, "Luke 1:39-56: Magnificat for a Broken World," *Huffington Post*, December 14, 2011, www.huffingtonpost.com/carolyn -sharp/luke-13956-magnificat-for_b_1146988.html?ir=Australia.
[2]Edwin Robertson, ed., *Dietrich Bonhoeffer's Christmas Sermons* (Grand Rapids: Zondervan, 2005). From a sermon from the third Sunday of Advent, December 17, 1933, on the Magnificat (Lk 1:46-55).
[3]Paul David Tripp, *Instruments in the Redeemer's Hands: People in Need of Change Helping People in Need of Change* (Phillipsburg, NJ: P&R Publishing, 2002).
[4]James Davison Hunter, *To Change the World: The Irony, Tragedy, and Possibility of Christianity in the Late Modern World* (New York: Oxford University Press, 2010), 234.
[5]Ibid., 4.
[6]Murray Bowen, *Family Therapy in Clinical Practice* (Lanham, MD: Rowman & Littlefield Publishers, 2004), 74.
[7]Neal Roese, *If Only: How to Turn Regret into Opportunity* (New York: Broadway, 2005), 169.
[8]For these and a host of other such stunts, see David Gibson, "Top 12 Pastor Stunts: Living as an Atheist Is Just the Latest Ministry Gimmick," January 14, 2014, https://sojo.net/articles/top-12-pastor-stunts-living -atheist-just-latest-ministry-gimmick.
[9]Seth Tower Hurd, "Do Church 'Publicity Stunts' Send the Wrong Message?," *Relevant*, October 9, 2014, www.relevantmagazine.com/god /church/do-church-publicity-stunts-send-wrong-message.
[10]Ibid.
[11]Thomas Moore, *Soul Mates* (New York: HarperCollins, 1994), viii.
[12]Anthony Smith, Facebook, June 16, 2016.

4 MIDWIVES TO THE BIRTH OF THE NEW CREATION

[1]Sheila Kitzinger, *Rediscovering Birth* (London: Pinter & Martin, 2011), 164.

[2]Catherine Pearson, "Midwifery Benefits? Improved Outcomes for Moms Who See Midwives, Review Finds," *Huffington Post*, August 21, 2013, www.huffingtonpost.com/2013/08/20/midwifery-benefits_n_3787058 .html.

5 MAKING SPACE FOR BIRTH TO HAPPEN

[1]Tom Kerns, "Socrates as Midwife," Philosophy 101, North Seattle Community College, http://philosophycourse.info/lecsite/lec-socmidwife .html.

[2]Ibid.

[3]Ibid.

[4]John B. Hayes, *Sub-merge: Living Deep in a Shallow World: Service, Justice and Contemplation Among the World's Poor* (Ventura, CA: Regal Books, 2006), 117.

[5]"Summary," *American Jerusalem: Jews and the Making of San Francisco*, www.americanjerusalem.com/story-summary.

[6]Thomas Troeger, *Imagining a Sermon* (Nashville: Abingdon Press, 1990).

[7]The fruits of all their efforts can be found here. Their report might inspire a similar exercise in your neighborhood. "Barneys Love Your Neighbour," www.barneys.org.au/wp-content/uploads/2014/12/LYNP-Booklet-for -web.pdf.

[8]Hayes, *Sub-merge*, 132.

[9]"Manly Heritage and History," Northern Beach Council: Manly, www .manly.nsw.gov.au/council/about-manly/manly-heritage-history.

[10]David Whyte, *Crossing the Unknown Sea: Work as a Pilgrimage of Identity* (New York: Riverhead Books, 2001), 109.

6 ON BEING ADAPTIVE AND DARING

[1]Walter Brueggemann, *Cadences of Home* (Louisville, KY: Westminster John Knox, 1997), 10.

[2]Ibid., 11.

[3]Cambridge Leadership Associates, "What Is Adaptive Leadership?" www.cambridge-leadership.com/adaptive-leadership.

[4]Eckhart Tolle, *A New Earth* (New York: Penguin, 2005), 274.

[5]From private correspondence. Used with permission.

[6]Ann Morisy, *Bothered and Bewildered* (London: Continuum, 2009).

[7]Richard Matheson, *Collected Stories, Vol. 1* (New York: Gauntlet Press, 2003), 93.

[8]Tim Dickau, *Plunging into the Kingdom Way: Practicing the Shared Strokes of Community, Hospitality, Justice, and Confession* (Eugene, OR: Cascade Books, 2011), 19.

[9]For more information on Makers Arcade see makersarcade.com.

7 HOW TO REALLY CHANGE THE WORLD

[1]Christopher Hitchens, *God Is Not Great* (New York: Hachette Book Group, 2007), 56.

[2]John Loftus, ed., *Christianity Is Not Great* (New York: Prometheus Books, 2014), 35.

[3]*Monty Python's Life of Brian*, directed by Terry Jones (London: Handmade Films, 1979).

[4]Jonathan Hill, *What Has Christianity Ever Done for Us?* (Oxford: Lion Hudson, 2005), 189.

[5]Ben Witherington III, *The Gospel of Mark: A Socio-Rhetorical Commentary* (Grand Rapids: Eerdmans, 2001), 172.

[6]The Social Ecological Model (SEM) is well known in social work ecosystems theory. This diagram can be found in many forms in many places. See, for example, www.esourceresearch.org/eSourceBook/Socialand BehavioralTheories/5InterventionstoChangeHealthBehavior/tabid/737 /Default.aspx.

[7]"Ideas and Examples of Early Practical Integration for CL Staff," Emory University, http://osls.emory.edu/files/leadership_emory_files/leadership _emory_staff/early_ideas_for_adoption.

[8]Ibid.

[9]"Social Change Model of Leadership," Emory University, osls.emory.edu /leadership_emory/our_philosphy/social_change.html.

[10]Attributed to Ed Stetzer in Dave Ferguson, "Explode Those Old Scoreboards," *Christian Standard*, May 10, 2015, christianstandard.com /2015/05/explode-those-old-scoreboards.

[11]Reggie McNeal, *Missional Renaissance* (San Francisco: Jossey-Bass, 2009), 68.

[12]Dave Ferguson, *Keeping Score: How To Know If Your Church Is Winning*, free ebook resource, Exponential Resources, https://exponential.org/resource-ebooks/keeping-score.

[13]Glenn Smith, "The Challenges of Urban Mission," *Lausanne World Pulse*, September 2006, www.lausanneworldpulse.com/themedarticles.php/480/09-2006.

[14]"Key Indicators of a Transformed City," Christian Direction Inc., Montreal, Quebec, http://direction.nationbuilder.com/12_indicators_of_a_transformed_city.

[15]Hill, *What Has Christianity Ever Done for Us?*, 29.

[16]Malcolm Gladwell, *David and Goliath* (New York: Penguin, 2009), 117.

8 CHANGING THE WORLD THROUGH OUR WORK

[1]C. J. Mahaney, Twitter, June 21, 2015.

[2]Paul Weston, compiler, *Lesslie Newbigin: Missionary Theologian: A Reader* (London: SPCK, 2006), 154-55.

[3]Lesslie Newbigin, *Foolishness to the Greeks* (Grand Rapids: Eerdmans, 1986), 140.

[4]Lesslie Newbigin, *The Other Side of 1984* (Geneva: World Council of Churches, 1990), 39.

[5]Amy L. Sherman, *Kingdom Calling* (Downers Grove, IL: InterVarsity Press, 2011), 100.

[6]Ibid., 99.

[7]Ibid., 108.

[8]Johannes Baptist Metz, *Theology of the World* (London: Herder and Herder, 1968), 90.

[9]David J. Bosch, *Transforming Mission* (Maryknoll, NY: Orbis, 1991), 153.

[10]Metz, *Theology of the World*, 92-93.

[11]Weston, *Lesslie Newbigin: Missionary Theologian*, 264.

[12]N. T. Wright, *Surprised by Hope* (New York: HarperCollins, 2008), 193.

[13]Andy Balch, private correspondence. Used with permission.

[14]*Luther's Works* (Philadelphia: Fortress, 1955–1986; 2009–), 6:407.22-23.

[15]*Luther's Works* 6:408.26-30.

[16]*Luther's Works* 6:409.7-10.

[17]Frederick Gaiser, ed., *Word & World*, vol. 25, no. 4 (fall 2005): 360.

18Mark Scandrette with Lisa Scandrette, *Free: Spending Your Time and Money on What Matters Most* (Downers Grove, IL: InterVarsity Press, 2013), 15.

19Franklin Graham, Facebook, March 31, 2015.

20For more information on ReWire see www.crmleaders.org/teams/rewire.

21"Loving a City Back to Life: A Visit with Craig Poole," www.youtube.com /watch?v=qRfae5EviHI.

9 CHANGING THE WORLD THROUGH PLACECRAFTING

1Image by Philip Straub featured on "Future City HD Wallpapers," accessed February 22, 2016, http://hdwallpaperbackgrounds.net/future-city-hd -wallpapers.

2N. T. Wright, *Surprised by Hope* (New York: HarperCollins, 2008), 265-66.

3Seah Chiang Nee, "Explaining the Ugly Singaporean," quoted in Lucky Tan, *Diary of a Singaporean Mind* blog, May 19, 2008, http://singapore mind.blogspot.com.au/2008/05/explaining-ugly-singaporean.html.

4UN Habitat issue paper, "Public Space," New York, May 2015, http:// unhabitat.org/wp-content/uploads/2015/04/Habitat-III-Issue-Paper-11 _Public-Space-2.0.compressed.pdf.

5Ethan Kent, "A Thriving Future of Places: Placemaking as the New Urban Agenda," www.pps.org/a-thriving-future-of-places-placemaking-as-the-new -urban-agenda/.

6Philip Sheldrake, *The Spiritual City* (Chichester, UK: John Wiley & Sons, 2014), 70-71.

7Mel McGowan, "Designing the Church as Today's Town Square," *Outreach Magazine*, June 28, 2015, www.outreachmagazine.com/ideas /12074-designing-the-church-as-todays-town-square.html.

8Ibid.

9Paul Sparks, Tim Soerens and Dwight J. Friesen, *The New Parish* (Downers Grove, IL: InterVarsity Press, 2014).

10Ibid., 47.

11Project for Public Spaces, "Eleven Principles for Creating Great Community Places," www.pps.org/reference/11steps/.

12Ibid.

13For more information, visit www.quartyardsd.com.

[14]Sean Benesh, *View from the Urban Loft* (Eugene, OR: Wipf and Stock Publishers, 2001).

[15]Eric O. Jacobsen, *The Space Between* (Grand Rapids: Baker Books, 2012), Kindle edition, Loc. 61.

[16]Project for Public Spaces, "Eleven Principles."

[17]Christopher J. H. Wright, *The Mission of God's People: A Biblical Theology of the Church's Mission* (Grand Rapids: Zondervan, 2010), 44.

[18]Project for Public Spaces, "Eleven Principles."

10 BEING CHANGED AS WE BRING CHANGE

[1]Roger Helland and Leonard Hjalmarson, *Missional Spirituality: Embodying God's Love from the Inside Out* (Downers Grove, IL: InterVarsity Press, 2011), 25-26.

[2]Jean Vanier, *Community and Growth, 2nd rev. ed.* (Mahwah, NJ: Paulist Press, 1989), 99.

[3]Evelyn Underhill, *Essential Writings* (Maryknoll, NY: Orbis, 2003), 31.

[4]Private correspondence. Used with permission.

[5]Jon Huckins with Rob Yackley, *Thin Places: Six Postures for Creating and Practicing Missional Community* (Kansas City, MO: House Studio, 2012).

[6]Christopher L. Heuertz, *Unexpected Gifts: Discovering the Way of Community* (New York: Howard Books, 2013), 194-95.

11 SUFFERING ALONG THE WAY

[1]Lesslie Newbigin, "What Is 'a Local Church Truly United'?," in *The Ecumenical Movement: An Anthology of Key Texts and Voices*, ed. Michael Kinnamon and Brian E. Cope (Grand Rapids: Eerdmans, 1996), 114.

[2]Ajith Fernando, "To Serve Is to Suffer," *Christianity Today*, July 20, 2010, www.christianitytoday.com/ct/2010/august/index.html.

[3]C. René Padilla, "Bible Studies," *Missiology* 10, no. 3 (1982): 338.

[4]*The Epistle of Mathetes to Diognetus*, in *The Ante-Nicene Fathers, Volume 1: The Apostolic Fathers with Justin Martyr and Irenaeus*, ed. Alexander Roberts, James Donaldson and Arthur Cleveland Coxe (New York: Cosimo Classics, 2007), 26-27.

[5]Megan Gandee, "'I'll Fight': 100 Years Since Booth's Final Address," *Doing the Most Good* (blog), Salvation Army, May 9, 2012.

[6]Kaj Munk, quoted in Thomas G. Long and Cornelius Plantinga Jr., eds., *A Chorus of Witnesses* (Grand Rapids: Eerdmans, 1994), 133.

ABOUT THE AUTHORS

Michael Frost is an Australian missiologist and one of the leading voices in the international missional conversation. He is the founding director of the Tinsley Institute, a mission study center at Morling College in Sydney, Australia. He is also a senior lecturer with the Melbourne University of Divinity. Frost is the author or editor of fifteen books, including the popular and award-winning titles *The Shaping of Things to Come* (2003), *Exiles* (2006), *The Road to Missional* (2011) and *Surprise the World!* (2016).

Christiana Rice is an on-the ground practitioner and visionary voice in the missional movement, serving as a coach and trainer with Thresholds (thresholdscommunity.org), a community of player-coaches who help people create spaces of discovery and communities of transformation. With her husband, Derek, she leads a neighborhood faith community in Golden Hill, San Diego. Christiana grew up in Tokyo, Japan, the daughter and grand-daughter of missionaries in that country. Whether teaching and coaching global leaders, engaging the deeper spiritual longings of her neighbors or embracing the sacred mundane of daily life with her family and her community, Christiana seeks to participate in God's restorative mission in all things. This is her first book.

IVP PRAXIS

EQUIPPING LEADERS FOR MINISTRY

"...TO EQUIP HIS PEOPLE FOR WORKS OF SERVICE,
SO THAT THE BODY OF CHRIST MAY BE BUILT UP."

EPHESIANS 4:12

God has called us to ministry. But it's not enough to have a vision for ministry if you don't have the practical skills for it. Nor is it enough to do the work of ministry if what you do is headed in the wrong direction. We need both vision *and* expertise for effective ministry. We need *praxis*.

Praxis puts theory into practice. It brings cutting-edge ministry expertise from visionary practitioners. You'll find sound biblical and theological foundations for ministry in the real world, with concrete examples for effective action and pastoral ministry. Praxis books are more than the "how to" – they're also the "why to." And because *being* is every bit as important as *doing*, Praxis attends to the inner life of the leader as well as the outer work of ministry. Feed your soul, and feed your ministry.

If you are called to ministry, you know you can't do it on your own. Let Praxis provide the companions you need to equip God's people for life in the kingdom.

www.ivpress.com/praxis

ALSO BY MICHAEL FROST

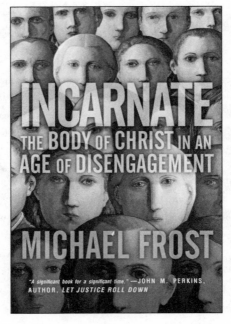

*Incarnate: The Body of Christ
in an Age of Disengagement*
978-0-8308-4417-3

Forge

The Forge Missions Training Network exists to help birth and nurture the missional church in America and beyond. Books published by InterVarsity Press that bear the Forge imprint will also serve that purpose.

Beyond Awkward, by Beau Crosetto

Creating a Missional Culture, by JR Woodward

Forge Guides for Missional Conversation (set of five), by Scott Nelson

Incarnate, by Michael Frost

The Missional Quest, by Lance Ford and Brad Brisco

More Than Enchanting, by Jo Saxton

Sentness, by Kim Hammond and Darren Cronshaw

The Story of God, the Story of Us (book and DVD), by Sean Gladding

---

For more information on Forge America, to apply for a Forge residency,
or to find or start a Forge hub in your area,
visit **www.forgeamerica.com**

For more information about Forge books from InterVarsity Press,
including forthcoming releases, visit **www.ivpress.com/forge**